DARE

Accepting the Challenge of Trusting Leadership

DARE

Accepting the Challenge of Trusting Leadership

Make your word good . . . and be as good as your word.

SCOTT WEISS

GREENLEAF
BOOK GROUP PRESS

Published by Greenleaf Book Group Press
Austin, Texas
www.gbgpress.com

Distributed by Greenleaf Book Group LLC

For ordering information or special discounts for bulk purchases, please contact Greenleaf Book Group LLC at PO Box 91869, Austin, TX 78709, 512.891.6100.

Design and composition by Greenleaf Book Group LLC
Cover design by Doug Foltz

Publisher's Cataloging-In-Publication Data
(Prepared by The Donohue Group, Inc.)
Weiss, Scott, 1959-
    Dare : accepting the challenge of trusting leadership / Scott Weiss.—1st ed.
    p. ; cm.
    "Make your word good . . . and be as good as your word."
    Issued also as an ebook.
    ISBN: 978-1-60832-422-4 (hardbound)
    1. Leadership. 2. Trust. I. Title.
HD57.7 .W45 2013
658.4/094   2012946899

Part of the Tree Neutral® program, which offsets the number of trees consumed in the production and printing of this book by taking proactive steps, such as planting trees in direct proportion to the number of trees used: www.treeneutral.com

TreeNeutral®

Printed in the United States of America on acid-free paper

13 14 15 16 17 18   10 9 8 7 6 5 4 3 2 1

First Edition

*This book is dedicated to the thousands of leaders
everywhere who dare to use trusting communication to lead
their teams and organizations.*

CONTENTS

Acknowledgments. . . . . **xi**

Chapter 1: A Crisis of Trust 1

Chapter 2: The Leadership Persona 7

The Fine Art of Deception 11

Perception Management 12

Eschewing Obfuscation. 15

Self-Deception and Collusion. 18

Business as Usual?. 22

DARE! 23

Chapter 3: What's Wrong with our Customers?. 25

The Customer Default Position. 27

The Customer Trust Position 32

DARE! 36

Chapter 4: Straight Talk to the Workforce. 39

Information Brokering 40

When the Truth Hurts 44

When We Don't Have the Answers 47

When We Fear Distracting the Workforce 49

DARE! 51

Chapter 5: New Values for Great Leaders 53
The Charismatic Leader. 55

The Self-Aware Leader 57

    Self-Reflection 65

    Vulnerability 68

    Honesty and Transparency 72

DARE! 75

Chapter 6: Customer Conversations 77
The Emotional Connection. 79

Faking Sincerity. 81

Transparency Not Optional. 85

Undercover Bosses 88

Raising the Bar 89

DARE! 91

Chapter 7: Trusting Corporate Cultures 93
The Open Communications Vision. 96

    Spreading the Word. 98

    Open in Name Only?. 99

Connectors in Chief 101

    Encouraging Introductions.. 102

    Connecting to the Community.. 102

    Monitoring Diversity Messaging. 104

    Embracing the Tools. 104

Making Face Time. 105

Setting the Example. 105

Safety Engineering .106

Expecting the Best 107

Modeling Authentic Conversations 108

Learning to Listen 109

Being Yourself. .111

Simple and Sincere 112

Choosing the Channel 113

Rewards and Recognition. 114

DARE! 117

Chapter 8: Is Business Evil?. 119

Must Business Do Good? 121

Doing Well While Doing Good 125

Being Good to Do Well. 126

Becoming as Good as Our Word 129

One Voice at a Time 131

ABOUT THE AUTHOR 133

ABOUT SPEAKEASY 135

NOTES 137

INDEX 141

ACKNOWLEDGMENTS

There are a number of individuals who I want to thank for their direct and indirect involvement in this book.

I offer first my heartfelt gratitude to my loving wife, Marci, and to my children, Alexandra, Monica, and Jake, who have always encouraged me to see the good in everyone and everything.

My deep appreciation goes out to my parents, Allen and Marilyn, who have instilled trust as the most important principle in any relationship, and to my brother, Steve, and my sister, Cathy, who as senior level executives model trust in their own communications and have served as great sources of inspiration.

I am especially grateful for the many mentors I've had throughout my life—extraordinary teachers and guides including Nory LeBrun, Terry McGuirk, Ted Turner, Sandy Linver, and Harold Berry, who have pushed me to be better.

Finally, my thanks must go to our extraordinary clients who contributed to this book, and my amazing team at Speakeasy, who dedicate their time and energy every day to changing the lives of others, from the inside out.

CHAPTER 1
A CRISIS OF TRUST

There's a crisis of trust in this country. You can see it everywhere you look. It's obvious in the abysmal approval rates for members of the U.S. Congress and our general distrust of elected officials at almost every level. It's evident, too, in the suspicion with which we view our financial and business leaders, our journalists, scientists, regulatory agencies, and educators—almost everyone, in fact, to whom we look for direction and leadership.

Frankly, we don't believe much, or believe *in* much, of anything anymore. Studies show that aside from a brief surge following September 11, 2001, trust in our institutions and one another has been steadily declining for forty years. For those of us who are old enough, just remembering the years of Vietnam, Watergate, junk bonds, Monica Lewinsky, Enron, and the Catholic Church sex scandals will explain some of that decline. But things haven't been much better for the generations following in our steps. From the disinformation that led us into the Iraq war to the string of financial scandals that wiped out billions in personal wealth to the house of toppling cards that became the worst recession in eighty years, our youth have suffered through more than a decade of almost unrelenting dishonesty.

The Baby Boomers, whose famous mantra was, "Don't trust anyone over thirty," may have been much more skeptical of their leaders and institutions than the WWII cohort that preceded them, but for today's young people, cynicism is the default position. With overwhelmingly negative views of government and institutions, business and the media, our Gen X, Y, and millenial youth could easily be labeled the "Jaded Generations."

There are various possible explanations for the generational component to this cynicism. Some of them go well beyond the scandals they've witnessed and the lies they've been sold. The rise of television and the internet certainly have a place in the equation. Cable and internet news sources now offer a multitude of digital journalists, bloggers, and pundits, all offering up opinions but diluting the authority of any individual voice. Where their parents and grandparents had only a few such authority figures, like Walter Cronkite, whose objectivity and integrity could be thoroughly trusted, today's youth have a cacophony of conflicting voices, all competing with their own versions of the truth.

Electronic and digital media may play other roles. Some theorists have suggested that the time devoted by the young to TV and internet pursuits may exacerbate isolation from larger institutions and traditional American culture. A series of focus groups conducted by Harvard University's Goodwork Project found that the teenagers they interviewed had an "overwhelming" distrust of the media, politicians, and the political process in general. Carrie James, research director for Goodwork, thinks that while these young people might trust family and close friends, "they don't have good mental models" of how to trust more distant figures.

Regardless of the complexity of the problem, the deep

cynicism of American youth is troubling. It suggests that their trust will be hard to recover. Given that these are tomorrow's leaders, one wonders when, and from where, their mental models for trustworthiness might emerge. One wonders whether our leaders and institutions can bring back the honesty, accountability, and transparency that will restore their faith, or whether the downward spiral of distrust will continue for each succeeding generation.

I'm not at all sure how we got here. I don't know how Americans became so familiar with deception that we almost expect it. I don't know exactly how the truth got such a bad reputation that we don't even strive for it anymore. I don't know when we came to assume that all communication must naturally be "spin" and every public speech a shallow grab for publicity. I'm not sure why so many of our business, government, and professional leaders have opted for policies that depend on feeding us misinformation, half-truths, and downright lies.

I am sure, however, about the ultimate consequences of those policies. Like everyone else, I'm witnessing them firsthand.

In the short run, and for a few individuals, companies, and institutions, these approaches may work. But in the long run, they won't. A foundation of trust is essential for all successful human interaction. It's the grease that facilitates social, political, and economic transactions of every type. To the extent that we are able to trust, we make friendships, enter into marriage and social bonds, and join groups. To the extent that trust diminishes risk and uncertainty, we create businesses and business partnerships, become loyal customers ourselves, and willingly and optimistically participate in our own democracy.

There are far-reaching sociological benefits to trust. The Pew

Research Center has found that in nations where trust is high, crime and corruption are low. The same principle operates in communities, in neighborhoods, in schools, and organizations. Much other research has demonstrated the self-perpetuating nature of trust and the reciprocal benefits that accrue to those who engage on its basis. Even in laboratory experiments, individuals who have been asked to engage in even the simplest trust-demanding transactions develop positive feelings toward their peers. Trust, apparently, begets trust. But the opposite is also true.

In the absence of trust, our elected leaders are unwilling to relinquish political power to those with opposing viewpoints, even for a short time. The resulting paralysis breeds more distrust, in the voting populace, among other nations, in those we trade with, and in those who finance our debt.

For business, trust may be the most critical value. It allows, of course, for the confidence to conduct our own day-to-day business transactions, but much more important, for faith in our institutions and economy at large. That faith is what allows us, as organizations but also as individuals, to plan for our futures, to think long term, to make investments or plant seeds for tomorrow with the expectation that we will see them flourish. When that foundation of trustworthiness erodes, as we've recently seen it crumbling beneath our financial systems, the result is profound confusion, a genuine sense of betrayal, and the feeling that somehow we've been robbed of our very future.

I've been concerned about this crisis in trust for some time, particularly as it relates to what I witness and experience every day. In our work at Speakeasy, we reach about five thousand individuals every year in twelve countries, from United Arab

Emirates to Vietnam. Our primary audience is corporate executives, but participants in our programs also include non-business professionals like athletes, teachers, doctors, clergy, government leaders, and authors. These are educated, articulate, and experienced leaders. They come to us initially believing that they are among the "good guys"—those enlightened individuals who stand outside and apart from the problems that have led to the pervasive cynicism that plagues our society. Yet many of them are surprised to learn that they themselves are part of the problem, not the solution. They are shocked to discover that in their own leadership practices they have been using their own voices to widen the credibility and confidence gap. They are surprised to learn that distrust is sown not just by criminality and outright fraud, but more insidiously by the varieties of deception that are part of every corporate toolbox.

We're justifiably proud of the work we do at Speakeasy and the numbers we reach. But in the face of this crisis we all need to do more. This book is my attempt to reach a larger audience—to do whatever I can to try to restore some of the sadly lacking trust that is creating this climate of uncertainty, suspicion, and stagnation.

If you are a leader with responsibility and influence, this book is addressed to you. If you are an executive leading a company, a manager leading a department, a pastor leading a church, a supervisor leading a shift of factory workers, a principal leading a school, these pages were written with you in mind. As the title suggests, they will ask you to accept a challenge, a "dare."

It's a simple challenge on its face, but one that seems extraordinarily difficult for many leaders to accept or even think about. Partially because it seems too simple. Mostly because it goes completely against the grain of what they believe a leader is. And that's not surprising. The attributes that my dare will ask you to develop are rarely found in executive boardrooms, the halls of government, or other chambers of power.

If you accept my challenge, you will be asked to rethink your entire concept of leadership, of power, and the responsibility of influence. You may be asked to tear down defense systems that you've spent a lifetime constructing.

DARE!

I dare you to be honest. To be authentic. To return transparency to your business and personal communications. To discover your true inner voice and become more of who you really are through your own spoken word. To make your word good, and become as good as your word.

I can promise that those of you who accept this challenge will reap surprising rewards both in your professional and personal lives. The results will be greater self-awareness, a more empathetic understanding of those around you, and more genuine connections and relationships with spouses, children, coworkers, and customers. You'll find renewed energy for the work that you do and a fuller realization of your true talents and potential.

I can make these outrageous promises because I know it works. For forty years, Speakeasy has witnessed the transformations that have occurred in the lives of those who dared to accept this challenge. We receive more than 1,500 letters, emails, and phone calls each year from individuals who have experienced these changes and are still excited about the rippling effects that continue in their professional and personal lives. I'm convinced that you can experience them too. I invite you to try. I dare you!

CHAPTER 2
THE LEADERSHIP PERSONA

In everyday usage, we think of a *persona* as an image or an impression. It's an image projected outward for social purposes or public consumption, designed to meet the demands of a given situation. Advertising and marketing experts create personas to represent an idealized customer or groups of potential buyers so that the company can focus its marketing efforts. In literature, a persona is an assumed identity, often an alter ego of the author. In drama, a persona is an actor in a play. In fact, the word's origin is from the Latin term for a theatrical mask.

We forget that sometimes. That a persona is not the genuine personality of an individual, but rather the mask that disguises it. Underneath that mask may be fears and insecurities that don't seem to fit the part we need to play. If we are in positions of leadership, we may be afraid of disappointing others. We may fear criticism or ridicule. We may be afraid that someone else will outperform or replace us if we appear weak, vulnerable, or emotional. We're better off, we think, with all that self-doubt concealed behind the masks. We can become very comfortable in those masks, and so convincing to others and ourselves in the roles we assume, that we become completely unconscious of playing a part. We forget that the actor in the center of the stage is not who we really are. And not someone we know, or even someone we really like, either.

My personal encounter with my own executive persona came as a life-changing shock. It occurred in December of 1994 as a result of a "DARE" from Sandy Linver to attend a communication development program at Speakeasy, a communications consulting firm she founded in Atlanta, Georgia. At thirty-five, I was already an executive vice president with Turner Broadcasting, overseeing two divisions and reporting directly to the second most senior executive who soon would be named the company's CEO. I believed that I was very much at the top of my game, already delivering a lot of high-level presentations, and getting consistent positive feedback. I was more than a little offended by the suggestion that I needed any help at all with my communication skills. But I went.

In Atlanta, I participated in Speakeasy's exclusive, invitation-only workshop for C-suite executives. Called "The Leader's Edge," this intense three-day workshop focused on communication style and delivery with respect to leadership. In spite of my initial resistance, I did my best to participate without revealing my conviction that I felt superior to this target audience that needed help with communication and presentation skills. I wasn't the least bit nervous when it came time to watch the video recordings of our individual presentations. I was sure I'd done just fine.

With the others in our group, I watched as the executive persona of Scott Weiss delivered his speech from the screen. The guy up there looked pretty good. Very sure of himself. Very corporate. Very buttoned up. I expected to be told, as I always had been before, that I was a very effective presenter. But after a moment, Sandy Linver, the faculty leader who had directed our session turned to ask me a question.

"So," she said, "as you look at yourself, objectively, how do you perceive this person?"

"Fine," I said. "He seems knowledgeable. Experienced. Very confident."

"Hmm," she said. "That's interesting. If you could separate yourself from this person and experience him objectively, would you want to hang out with a person like that on the weekend?"

It was a strange question. But I looked at that person frozen on the TV monitor and thought about it. Reluctantly, I had to tell the truth.

"No," I said. "Probably not."

"Really?" she asked. "And why not?"

"Well," I said, "because I don't hang out with people like that."

I'm not sure whether there was a collective gasp from the audience or just a stunned silence, but what she said next definitely stunned me.

"You know, don't you, that you're talking about *yourself?*"

Yes. I was. I had just admitted that the person I was projecting was not someone to whom I could relate. He wasn't even someone I really liked!

And apparently, I wasn't the only one to be put off by Scott Weiss's executive persona. In our remaining time together, other members of the audience began to offer more specific impressions of how they had experienced me as a communicator, and as a person.

Arrogant.
Cocky.
Superior.
Disconnected.
Not real.

Those were just some of the terms they used. I had never heard myself described this way before. I felt like the emperor with no clothes.

I had not gone to Speakeasy for a consciousness-raising experience. But I sure had one. In the weeks following that close and uncomfortable encounter with my own executive persona, I did a lot of thinking. I examined what I had learned about how others actually *did* experience me, and thought about how I *wanted* people to experience me. There was a gaping abyss between those two extremes, and I realized that I had a lot of work to do to bring them closer together—to become more congruent as an individual and as a leader. I needed to find my authentic self and learn how to bring more of my real personality to my vocation.

After several months of introspection and self-reflection, I ultimately came to realize that my current environment was not going to be supportive of the changes I wanted to make. In 1995, I left Turner to join Speakeasy and pursue what has become my life's work. I was very fortunate that Sandy Linver took me under her wing and gave me the opportunity to begin learning how to drop my own masks and help others to do the same. Under her tutelage, I spent the next ten years studying and being relentlessly guided and re-directed to think about how I wanted to be experienced as a person, not just as an executive. I took retreats away from family and friends to work on my own self-awareness, and generally spent countless hours focused on my own "becoming."

It was not an easy process, but for me it was not just valuable, but necessary. In 2004, I bought the company and became president and CEO.

I share this story almost every day with leaders who are unaware that they are communicating to the world from behind a mask. For many, that realization comes as an uncomfortable epiphany. It certainly did for me. But it can also mark the beginning of a remarkable and transformative journey, one that is as much about personal growth as it is about communication. It has to start with self-awareness, and a willingness to examine the ways that we as leaders deceive others and ourselves.

The Fine Art of Deception

Most executives get very defensive when confronted with the word "lie" in any context. They would never see themselves as liars or admit that they ever lie. To be fair, the overwhelming majority of our nation's top leaders are individuals who conduct themselves with honesty and integrity. Very few of us tell the Bernie Madoff, Ken Lay, or Jeffrey Skilling kind of lies. And this is not a book about securities fraud or accounting malfeasance. It's not about the big black lies driven by pure ego and unbridled greed. To some extent, however, it is about deception. It's about the commonplace, but wholly unnecessary, deceptions committed in the vast gray area between polite white lies and the horrendously malicious fabrications that make headline news. It's about the deceits we practice on our customers, our employees, and ourselves in the name of "business as usual."

I'm concerned about the many well-meaning, otherwise highly ethical leaders who may not even be conscious of how commonplace these deceptions have become or how routinely they're practiced. To the world at large, in our external corporate communications and marketing, we have become all too casual about encouraging deception through exaggeration and "spin." In our internal communications, inside the walls of our own organizations, we cloud our intentions with corporate-speak and euphemism. We feel little obligation to speak honestly and openly to our own employees and operate to a great extent as though our business was none of their business. At the personal level, we engage from behind false personas and co-opt others into deceptions that rob us of self-awareness, more genuine relationships, and personal and professional growth.

These types of deceit are not intended to harm others. They're not consciously meant to defraud, defame, or cheat. But I believe that they exact a significant price. I think the costs are greater than most people imagine. While hard to calculate, they manifest in an unengaged workforce and higher employee turnover, in lower earnings related to lost time, creativity, and innovation, and especially in the valuable commodity of public trust.

Perception Management

For the external world, our communications are usually highly structured. These are often occasioned by the need for press releases or public pronouncements, or by very large and important formal meetings with customers, bankers, or shareholders. We're very careful about managing these big, public communications. We spend a lot of time, and often a lot of money, crafting their content, trying to put the best face on these high stakes messages so that financial analysts, the press, stakeholders, and shareholders will have confidence in our current endeavors and future direction. Entire industries exist to help us with this "perception management"—a term coined by the U.S. military, now commonly understood as a synonym for persuasion. Originally intended, and still defined, by the Department of Defense as persuasion limited to foreign audiences, perception management is now an advertised service offered by public relations firms for audiences of all types. It's a public relations task that at its very core assumes massive deception.

The job of perception management becomes especially important when the "facts on the ground," to use the military expression, are hard to put a good face on. The task then may even require the creation of new facts that can be sold as truth— the invention of a new and more attractive reality, created by media, to replace or distract from the unpleasant one. At the very least, perception management requires "spinning" the truth. This may involve putting more emphasis on your own side of the story while de-emphasizing material information. (Recall BP's CEO Bob Dudley announcing BP's safest decade in history, after the Deep Horizon oil spill.) It may require reorganizing or selectively interpreting data. The tobacco industry used this technique masterfully for decades, and we've seen it at work also in the slow, statistic-clouded investigations surrounding automobile recalls. We have the new terms "greenwashing" and "pinkwashing" to describe the practices of erroneously promoting perceptions of an organization's aims and policies as environmentally friendly or pro-woman.

Sometimes the perception management strategy calls for shifting the blame. We saw this strategy in full force during the recent financial collapse. At companies like Goldman Sachs, the executives and fund managers, who had ignored risk management policies in favor of revenues and bonuses, shifted blame to mortgage brokers. These brokers then sold loans to unqualified buyers in order to collect more commissions, only to later blame those same homeowners for buying homes they couldn't afford.

Perception management for business is founded on the commonly held view that all external communication is marketing, and that business is a game. According to the rules of the game, deceptions that would be unacceptable in everyday life are not merely acceptable, but to be expected. *Caveat emptor* is the prevailing principle and for the most part, a sophisticated public goes along. At least until we're harmed. When we're injured or cheated, we erupt into moral outrage and demand to know why we were lied to.

This double standard enables what psychologists David Messick and Ann Tenbrunsel call "ethical fading"—the process by which the moral colors of an ethical decision fade into bleached hues that are void of moral implications.[1] Through this slow erosion of ethical standards, we become habituated to, and participate in, behaviors we would never consciously condone. Ethical fading may explain how so many Arthur Andersen accountants could have failed to observe or react to the ongoing transgressions at Enron. It sheds light on the slow emergence of whistleblowers in fiascos like the phone-hacking scandal surrounding News Corp. It explains a lot about how many recent ethics scandals became so complex, endured so long, and involved so many "honest" individuals before making the evening news.

 Those who think it permissible to tell white lies soon grow color blind.
—Austin O'Malley

Our large public audiences, however, aren't the only ones whose perceptions we try to manage and on whom we practice deception. Within the corporate compound itself, our communications create thick clouds of obscurity. We are much less conscious of creating this fog. We are less deliberate about it, and usually manage it without paying outside consultants. But it, too, becomes a smokescreen to conceal, distract, and confuse.

Eschewing Obfuscation

In our internal communications, which take place in the offices and conference rooms where the real, day-to-day work of business gets done, we might be expected to be far more authentic. In this environment, however, the situation isn't much better. In reality, our meetings are often robotic stage plays scripted from arbitrary bullet-point agendas, delivered with little energy, and almost evasive in their lack of eye-to-eye contact. We flood our audiences with information, bombarding them with metrics, bar graphs, pie charts, and PowerPoint slides by the hundreds. Our internal reports and memoranda, even our emails, are obscured by euphemisms, an alphabet soup of acronyms, empty catchphrases, and meaningless clichés. We "synergize strategic perspectives" and "shift paradigms." We "downsize," "right size," "outplace," and make "workforce adjustments," but we don't fire anybody anymore. We "collaborate" and "interface" with coworkers, but rarely have a simple, honest conversation with them.

Every industry, of course, is inclined to develop its own jargon as verbal shorthand. And euphemisms can be useful metaphors for simplifying complex ideas. But there is much more going on here than a desire for simple economy in communication.

Language euphemisms allow us to re-label morally questionable actions as benign or socially acceptable. We can discuss "collateral damage" without thinking about civilian deaths, and condone "aggressive" accounting practices without admitting they're illegal. We become habituated to these linguistic disguises and unconscious of the ethical fading taking place. As Tenbrunsel and Messick point out,

> Metaphors such as "pro forma," "creative accounting," and "rightsizing" can be so commonplace that we no longer see the questionable behavior they were designed to disguise. Perhaps worse, the metaphors can be dangerously transformed from descriptions to explanations. In doing so, unethical behavior becomes justifiable through a process of deception, in which we transform morally wrong behavior into socially acceptable actions.[2]

Beyond its value for hiding what we're doing, inflated and obscure language has other uses. It can also be used as a technique for intimidation. The assumption here is that if others don't understand what we're talking about, we're not likely to be challenged. Our ability to talk over their heads must come from superior education or knowledge, justifying our titles or compensation. It demonstrates how smart we are, why we belong in the position we're in, or why we should be considered for a promotion. It's a way of positioning ourselves at the top of the corporate food chain.

The classic illustration of just how effective this type of deception can be comes from the hoax pulled off by mathematician Alan Sokal in 1996. Sokal wrote a paper entitled, "Transgressing the Boundaries: Toward a Transformative Hermeneutics of Quantum Gravity," which he submitted for publication to a prestigious academic journal. The paper was pure gibberish, fashioned by Sokal from grandiose language and the fashionable scientific jargon of the time, but it was accepted for publication.[3]

While this example comes from academia, there are few of us who haven't walked away from a business meeting or conference at one point in time scratching our heads and at least secretly wondering, "What the hell did he *say*?" It's not hard at all to imagine Sokal's hoax being perpetrated on a business school or providing a chapter in an MBA textbook.

When "corporate speak" emanates from the top, it is mimicked and relayed by middle management to subordinates all the way down the chain until the entire organization's communication culture reflects a lack of authentic dialog. Teams may leave meetings nodding their heads, but little relevant information or actionable direction has actually penetrated the fog. And they haven't been infected with the slightest contagion of excitement or enthusiasm for whatever the project involves.

While I hate to dispute an old saw, this kind of talk is not cheap. These breakdowns in communications have real financial consequences. And yet those consequences are rarely exposed or acknowledged. I frequently have discussions with leaders who are troubled after the failure of an important initiative. When I question them about what they believe were the causes of this failure, they often bring out a laundry list of excuses.

"The economy is just too soft."
"There wasn't enough marketing."
"The growth projections were off."
"We were out-priced, or over-packaged."
"The distributors delayed us."
"Fuel costs went up."

Almost never do I hear "communication" named as a contributing factor, or hear these leaders themselves taking any responsibility for their own part in the failure. I don't, for example, often hear leaders make admissions like

"I failed to provide concise, motivating direction to my teams."

"I failed to compel customers or clients to do business with us."

"I failed to communicate my personal passion about this opportunity to the organization."

"I failed to communicate a common goal—to articulate to others what was in it for them, and how we'd all benefit from this effort."

These very same leaders may be acknowledged masters at other functions of management. They may be very good at planning, defining goals, setting measurable targets, and other established fundamentals of business success. But they undervalue communication—the very cord that ties all of these other skills together. While they may be paying a great deal of attention to the "perception management" aspect of communication for stockholders and the public, they're all but oblivious to the poor quality and diminished clarity of the organization's internal communications. And they deceive themselves as to the role of their own leadership in this costly, time-consuming failure.

Self-Deception and Collusion

In the discussion thus far, I've devoted considerable attention to the deceptions we perpetrate in our communications to public audiences and to the internal audiences within our own organizations. The most important audience of all, however, is our innermost selves. To the extent that we deceive this primary audience, we deprive ourselves of growth in both our professional and personal lives.

The only cure for self-deception is self-awareness. It's consciously choosing to explore the unknown territory of the inner self. But corporate America erects many obstacles to taking that journey into the self and little encouragement to do so. Long-standing traditions of autocracy and hierarchy serve to isolate executives and increase the distance they must overcome to achieve genuine relationships. The demands on our time don't leave much room for self-reflection, and hard-driving, results-oriented personalities aren't expected to be introspective anyway. As was my own case, our executive persona may present an air of confidence, superiority, and dominance that discourages meaningful interactions. Our leadership style has worked well so far. There's no incentive for taking off the mask and revealing weakness, insecurity, or doubt.

To make difficult matters worse, our own peers and coworkers may discourage us from appearing vulnerable or discovering our own weaknesses. Others are drawn into a collusion that benefits no one and makes change difficult.

I witness ineffective delivery from the C–Suite on a regular basis and see this collusion in action. Recently I observed a CEO address a conference as a keynote speaker. He delivered a truly insipid, uninspiring presentation, rife with buzzwords, euphemisms, and clichés. Yet somehow, his performance was rewarded by a standing ovation, initiated and encouraged by a front row filled with his loyal staff.

This collusion might not seem detrimental at first, but consider that the speaker walked away from the experience thinking he had just hit a home run, when in fact he totally struck out.

What his team needed was a great corporate leader and communicator, but somewhere along the way he had co-opted subordinates into helping him shore up his self-deception. The result was missed opportunities for the company, missed opportunities for the team, and the loss for that executive of an opportunity for professional growth.

Corporate America has long fostered a "kissing up" culture. I don't expect, in this economy, that the situation is getting any better. The need for job security and the hopes of a promotion or more money are powerful incentives for flattering the boss—especially when that boss is disconnected from the impact of his or her actions on others and has made it clear that flattery will get you everywhere.

 Suppose we were able to share meanings freely without a compulsive urge to impose our view or conform to those of others and without distortion and self-deception. Would this not constitute a real revolution in culture?
—David Bohm

The history of American enterprise is littered with examples of fortunes lost and lives damaged because subordinates were afraid to challenge the mediocre (or really bad) ideas of their leaders. There's a tremendous waste of financial as well as human resources in atmospheres that don't foster cooperation and honest feedback. Creativity is discouraged and innovation stifled. The cycle of cynicism and distrust is perpetuated.

For leaders themselves, the personal costs of self-deception can also be high. When our leadership personas and our real personalities are out of sync, we can experience an uncomfortable disconnection. When our corporate self speaks and behaves in an entirely different manner, embraces an entirely different ethical system, and is effectively walled off from genuine interaction with others, there are bound to be consequences. When each Monday morning finds us becoming someone we would never want to have a beer with on Saturday afternoon, the result can be inner turmoil.

This lack of congruence feeds anxiety and stress. At the highest levels, and in the worst cases, this disconnect can lead to depression and dysfunction. It can be especially damaging in family and personal relationships with those who are only privy to the private, unmasked personality and can't comprehend the stresses of a double life. The common management injunction, "Don't bring it home," reveals this duality. Even the simple stresses of keeping our masks in place can be psychologically draining.

Arto Kuusinen, who is an executive partner with Accenture, is one of the enlightened leaders who has discovered that hiding behind that mask, or to use his metaphor, that "smoke screen," can be stressful:

> By nature we are seeking respect and acceptance. That's one of the drivers for us to communicate only part of ourselves or part of the story. We're afraid of exposing ourselves, so we build up a "smoke screen" to hide parts of the story we want to hide. I have mastered numerous smoke screens in order to seek respect and acceptance.
>
> But this kind of communication behavior really builds up your stress level. Your unconscious mind knows you are hiding things on purpose, and you're afraid of clearing out your smoke screen as it will expose your vulnerability.

An alternative communication behavior I have tried to exercise is based on full transparency and honesty—not hiding anything. I've found that whatever you leave out or behind you, you will find it in front of you one of these days anyway. There is no place you can park all the things you want to keep behind your smoke screen. One day, even the most dense fog will clear out.

Arto's words reveal not only the strains of masking or smoke screening, but also the likely futility of it. Even in the best-handled cases, this lack of congruence drains energy and enthusiasm—the passion that enables us not just to survive, but also to thrive in our vocations.

Business as Usual?

Is this really just business as usual? Must we resign ourselves to the notion that external communication is mere manipulation—a con job on those who buy from or invest in us? Is it a necessary given that our meetings and internal communications must be clouds of obscurity? Is it just naïve to think business messaging even has a moral component?

Or is there another way?

Could enlightened leadership help us foster a revolution in bringing word and deed closer together? Could the examples of honest, courageous leaders challenge the assumption that business ethics are qualitatively different from human ethics? Could business leaders begin closing the trust gap that business itself has helped to create?

> **In a time of universal deceit, telling the truth is a revolutionary act.**
> **—George Orwell**

I do think this is possible. I'm convinced that the truth can again become an essential business value. I believe very strongly that the job of professional communication consultants should be to assist and encourage clients to tell the truth—not to teach them how to spin or dissemble it. I am naïve enough to believe that the trust fall can be slowed, or reversed, if leaders are willing to make the truth their competitive advantage.

From my own experience, and what I have learned from many I've worked with, I know that if we are honest and forthright with that most primary, all-important audience of ourselves, our communication to the rest of the world becomes, if not always easy, at least authentic. Our messaging then comes from our true inner voice. That's the voice that will stir people, inspiring them to act, to believe, even to change.

DARE!

Having the courage to look behind our own masks is the first step toward enlightened leadership. If we are to be leaders who are genuinely trusted, we are obliged to risk a journey into our inner selves. That journey requires thinking about the roles we play and the persona we project. It means examining the elements of that persona that feel uncomfortable, false, or alien.

It may demand asking difficult questions and confronting unpleasant answers. Do I dare to take a hard look at the communication styles, even the vocabulary, within my own organization? Am I willing to take personal responsibility for our failures in communication? Do I actively solicit honest feedback, or do my own subordinates feel unsafe in disagreeing with me?

Finally, do I even *dare* to be as truthful, honest, and transparent as I can be? Can I lead from such an ethical stance?

CHAPTER 3

WHAT'S WRONG WITH OUR CUSTOMERS?

American consumers have been in a very bad mood lately. They seem angrier than ever before. They're increasingly vocal and ever more activist. They're prone to organize themselves into groups to magnify their discontent and to find ways to boycott our companies or our brands. Sometimes they actually bully us into changing policies or practices that weren't really on the agenda (like when they bullied Bank of America into backing down on that measly little five-buck debit card charge). And sometimes they're just a nuisance (like when they hijacked the Twitter hashtag for BlackBerry manufacturer RIM to vent their frustrations with the tech company). Either way, they're really throwing their weight around these days. We're finding it harder to ignore them. And they're putting a lot of pressure on our media spin staff.

Consumers just don't seem satisfied anymore with being able to compare prices and product attributes in minutes. (This development, as you know, hasn't been so great for business.) These customers of ours have become terrible busybodies in general. They've developed all manner of new, and rather unreasonable, expectations about the nature of the buying relationship and are sticking their noses into places where they don't belong. Now, for the price of a widget, they think they're entitled to opinions on everything from our executive compensation packages to our corporate citizenship. They're questioning our HR policies, our management styles, our corporate investments, our use of resources—all manner of "values" that have nothing to do with widgets.

Some experts believe that the bad-mood pendulum will soon swing back. Certainly, the series of scandals that have rocked the U.S. economic system, the painful recession, and the still-sluggish recovery have taken a toll. It's only natural that our customers would be retrenching, economizing, maybe running a little scared right now. But consumers have always been a little skeptical, haven't they? The job crisis and depleted levels of disposable income, while grim, are only temporary setbacks for American business. These factors exaggerate the normal, only slightly suspicious nature of our clients and customers. When the economy improves, we'll be back to business as usual.

Don't believe it. I certainly don't. I think that a seismic change has taken place. The state of trust between the nation's businesses and its customers has been deeply, pervasively damaged. Lev Janashvili, writing early in 2012 for *PRWeek*, also sees the consumer mood as much more than the mere reflection of a temporary economic cycle:

> In aggregate, we see clear and convincing evidence of the sorry state of trust. These are not outlying data points that capture bursts of skepticism and anger. These are not negligible downticks that punctuate an otherwise healthy trend. These are

not "normal" cycles of discontent that rise and fall with the rise and fall of good things such as economic growth and bad things such as unemployment. Most recent confidence, trust, or reputation surveys represent snapshots of multi-year or multi-decade descents into broad-based "structural" distrust.[4]

The "structural" distrust to which Janashvili refers suggests that the very fundamentals of the buyer/seller relationship have changed. Our customers are now looking at us through a new lens that finds and magnifies our smallest flaws. They're not just on to us, they're hyper-conscious of the full range of deceptions of which we've proved capable. It may, as the reputation surveys seem to show, take many years, or many decades, to restore much of the trust that a few businesses have forfeited on behalf of us all. But our customers are not likely to ever return to the state of naiveté that prevailed before Enron became a household word. Consciousness, once raised, can never be lowered.

The Customer Default Position

Where *do* our customers begin in this new environment of deepened distrust and cynicism? How *do* they approach commerce in a very bad mood? I think I know. I know, because like every CEO, president, owner, or manager of any organization, large or small, I'm also a customer myself.

Let's imagine that I'm John Q. customer. Assume that I'm considering whether to take a chance on doing business with your company. I may have heard of your products, services, or organization, but I've yet to become your customer. We don't yet have a relationship. Here's my starting point—the set of attitudes and perceptions I'm most likely to bring to the process. These are the hurdles of doubt and mistrust that I'll have to get over before I sign on the dotted line or plunk down my cash or credit card.

1. I don't believe your marketing or advertising.

Oh, sure, I've noticed your ads. They're slick, or loud, or so ubiquitous that I couldn't miss them. I'm in the market for what you're selling, so something there caught my eye, attracted my attention, or piqued my curiosity. I'm considering. But like most other customers today, I'm a thoroughgoing cynic when it comes to marketing. Forrester's data shows that only 6 percent of us think that companies generally tell the truth in advertising.

As for myself, I'm almost inured to the hype and the hyperbole, the spurious claims, and the sales speak. For the most part, I dismiss it. You don't speak to me personally. I don't hear a human voice. You're interested in selling products and services to me, but not necessarily the product or service that's right for me.

Of course you say you can give me the best quality, the finest service, and the lowest price, but I know that no one can offer all three. I've just got to figure out where the real manipulation will take place. My default position is suspicion.

2. I don't consider you the authority.

When seeking a credible source of information on your company or product, like most potential customers, I'm going to seek the advice of others first. You see that I'm doing this a lot now in the explosion of user-generated ratings, rankings, and reviews that have pervaded social media and the internet. When

I want to know something about you, I'll ask an outsider. Probably someone I know. But sadly, as the Edelman Trust Barometer has shown, I'm far less likely to believe your company's employees, public relations people, celebrities, or you, the CEO (in that descending order). As a matter of fact, my belief in CEO credibility dropped twelve points this year, to 38 percent, the biggest drop in trust in U.S. history.[5] Maybe I have a little confidence in your employees. But you? Not so much.

 Don't blame the marketing department. The buck stops with the chief executive.
—**John D. Rockefeller**

3. I don't expect that you will stand by your product or service.

Should I decide to do business with you, I'm prepared for something to go wrong and I don't have a lot of confidence that you'll make it right. I may have missed something in that microscopic print that protects you, not me, and I'll feel a little foolish. I'm pretty sure, too, that our customer service encounters are going to be a hassle. Should I call your Customer Service Center, I fully expect to be greeted by a recording, put on hold, and forced to spend time listening to canned music or canned sales spiels. You'll be telling me that my call is very important to you, but I won't be feeling important. I'll feel naïve and incompetent. And stressed.

While research shows that the most important attributes for complaining customers are the contact employees' authenticity, competence, and active listening skills, I don't expect to encounter those attributes. My experience with contact employees has led me to believe that they don't really take me seriously and they don't really care. Maybe they're stressed, too. In all likelihood they're being monitored, timed, and quantified. They're trained to read from scripts and do "complaints by the numbers," but they're not empowered to speak to me authentically or take any personal initiative to solve my problem. I get it. I've been there before.

4. I will tell eleven other people about a bad experience with your product or service.

If you let me down, you can expect me to share the details of my experience, my opinion of your company, and the way it treated me. I'll tell my family and friends by word of mouth, so that they won't repeat my mistake, but the internet makes it easy for me to spread the word to strangers, too. I may spread it widely and I may do it with a vengeance. I'll complain on my blog, on consumer and user websites, on my own Facebook page, and definitely on yours. If I'm really mad, like Dave Carroll was when United Airlines broke his guitar and wouldn't take responsibility, maybe I'll post a YouTube video. Who knows? Maybe my audience of eleven could balloon to 150,000.[6]

Can you blame me? Perhaps I haven't been injured outright. But I've been insulted and humiliated. You've taken my time and you've taken my money. I'm in a bad mood and I need to vent.

5. I don't expect that our relationship will last.

I may be willing to take a chance on this initial arrangement, but I'm not terribly optimistic that we'll be starting a long-term relationship. Every transaction these days feels like a gamble and the odds seem stacked against me. Odds are I'll be disappointed. I'll have to start all over again, naively searching for a company I can really trust.

6. My perception of your company is not good.

I don't know you yet, but I've lived through this recession. I remember the scandals. I read the news. Especially if your company is a large one, I imagine that it's like most corporations— a greedy, soulless, monolith interested only in profit. You don't really care about me, about the environment, or about any of the social ills that plague our society. You're driven solely by quarterly sales figures and stock price increases. You just want my money.

Maybe I'm not being fair to you. I really don't know much about your organizational values or your concept of corporate citizenship. You don't seem to be communicating them very well or running the risk of tying your product to principles. I'm in a bad mood these days and maybe it really isn't your fault that I'm judging you *de facto*. But your reputation, by association, has been tarnished by some pretty ugly mischief in the last few years. Until I know you better, I'm tarring you with the same brush.

7. I simply don't trust you.

I just don't.

There. That's where I am when I begin to consider doing business with you. That's my starting place, my default position. Whether you call it cynicism or sophistication, it's pretty much where we all start. *Buyer beware*, we're told. And so we are. Wary. Suspicious. Distrustful.

But the truth is that we don't necessarily enjoy this state of affairs. A growing body of research hints that humans are hardwired to trust. While we don't want to trust blindly, or be made fools of over our misplaced faith, the science of trust suggests that humans want to trust, even need to trust. We want to feel the positive emotions that engaging in trusting transactions engenders in us and we want to feel less anxiety as customers and consumers. Given a choice, we'd rather trust.

The Customer Trust Position

Here's a different list of facts which parallels, and *seems* to contradict, the first one. It really doesn't. There's really no cause for cognitive dissonance here at all. This second list is just as true as the first one. The difference is a matter of perspective—a subtle shift that emphasizes not our consumer's bad mood, but our innate desire to trust. Here's the Customer Trust Position, starting with a different set of assumptions about the buyer/seller relationship.

1. As your potential customer, I *want* to believe that your advertising is truthful and that your marketing messages are honest and sincere.

I really would like to believe that your product or service will deliver as advertised. And why shouldn't I? Do any of us really enjoy the prospect of being deceived? I'm willing to read, or to listen to, your sales pitch, your guarantees, and all of the marketing messages that might affect my decision. I'll examine them, to the best of my ability, for those places where you might deceive me, but I'm also listening for the ring of truth. That's what I really hope to hear. You should know that I *want* to believe. I need to think that I'm about to embark on a fair, honest, and truthful relationship.

And should you prove to me, even once, that you're as good as your word, I'm likely to believe what you say in the future. For your company, as least, the default position will have been switched over to trust.

2. I really *want* to turn to you for credible information on your own product or service.

In theory, you're the ones who should know the most, aren't you? You should be able to provide me with the quickest, safest, or most economical solution. It would save me a lot of time and energy if I could just get sound knowledge, a fast answer, or a quick fix from you in the first place. It would be nice, too, if you'd volunteer information about the design flaws, the fine print exclusions, the missing features, the safety concerns, and the extra charges. Heck, I'd even like you to tell me the competitor's cheaper alternative!

I'd like to be able to read and understand your product instructions, and it would be great, too, should you find me out there on the Web, struggling to find answers to my questions, if you would reach out to me. Maybe you could use social media to extend a helping hand.

If I have to ask outsiders, I will. But I would rather ask you, and I'd really appreciate it if you were truthful with me, and forthrightly transparent about what I don't know, but you do.

3. I really *want* to believe that you will stand behind what you sell.

I would really like to believe that doing business with you is more than a calculated gamble. I'd like to know that your warrants and guarantees are not just words around loopholes, but real promises you're making to me. Ones you intend to keep.

I want to discover your user-friendly Customer Service site with its great knowledge base and its thorough, honest, and transparent discussion of issues. I want to expect a real human being at the end of the line at your Call Center, one who takes me seriously, cares about my problem, and has the authority to make it right.

I like to be pleasantly surprised by the ease of exchanges or refunds. This gives me confidence to buy from you again.

I do realize that sometimes things will go wrong between us. But that won't necessarily end our relationship. When you treat me courteously and go out of your way to make it right, my faith in the integrity of at least one business will be restored. You will have taught me to trust you, and I'll be much more likely to buy from you again.

4. I will tell at least *six* people about how happy I am with your product or service.

That's a lot of free advertising. And when I'm happy I can be very enthusiastic. I can be downright evangelical. Perhaps I'm not as likely to do you as much potential good here as I am to do you harm when things go badly between us, but I'm actually pleased to recommend a nice restaurant, a good insurance agent, or my favorite brand of shoes to friends or family who solicit my opinion. And sometimes, on the internet, I just want to brag about a great deal or an extraordinary customer service experience.

Make me happy and I'll become your company's vocal, energetic sales rep. For free!

5. I'd really *love* to have a long-term relationship with you.

Contrary to what you may think, your own goals here are completely aligned with mine. You find it much more economical to resell, cross-sell, and upsell to me than to start all over again with a brand new customer. And I'd like to put to rest at least a few of my endless searches for best fit, good quality, good performance, and good price.

I'm not as capricious as you seem to think I am. I like having my good judgment confirmed and knowing that my trust wasn't misplaced. I'd like to think that we could get comfortable with each other and that I can be loyal to your brand. I'd really *like* to buy from you again. And again, and again, and again.

6. I really *want* to hold a positive image of your organization.

I'd really be much happier doing business with the "good guys." I'd like to think that you're working for solutions and not just creating problems for everyone but your stockholders. I'd like to support a company whose values are in alignment with my own and with most of society's. I'll even pay a little more for products that are produced ethically, by companies who treat their employees well and who channel some of their energies and resources into a cause I can get behind.

It's much easier for me now to investigate a company's reputation and discover the parent companies of brands. I'm interested in where those companies operate, who they have injured or offended, and what causes they have supported. I don't have any trouble boycotting a product on the basis of a company's reputation, and research shows I'm not alone. No less than 70 percent of consumers have actively avoided a product because of its parent company.[7]

It's much easier for me to believe in you, and to make a highly emotional connection to your brand or service, if I know that your company has a conscience. I have to buy from someone, after all. Let me take part in the solutions, too.

7. I *want* to trust you.
Please don't make it hard.

DARE!
My dare for this chapter is simple. For a few moments I'd like you to put your leadership hat aside and only wear the one that every single one of us dons at least hundreds, perhaps thousands, of times each year. Be just a consumer. A customer. It should be easy to think like one and feel like one because you *are* one, all the time. Next, I dare you to recall the last time that a transaction—for tennis shoes, an insurance policy, a vacation, or a piece of software—left you more than dissatisfied. Think about a time that you felt especially betrayed, misled, or cheated. Recall your

anger, your frustration, and your embarrassment. I dare you to deny that the experience left you with a generally diminished capacity for trust. In insurance companies or tennis shoe manufacturers, certainly. But also in your fellow man.

When you've marinated in that unpleasant memory for a bit, I'd like you to put your leadership hat back on. Think about your organization's own customers or clients. Reflect on the way you market, warrant, serve, and generally communicate to them. Are you 100 percent confident that your own organization's actions are working to reset the customer default position to trust?

CHAPTER 4
STRAIGHT TALK TO THE WORKFORCE

There's a great deal of emphasis these days on how globalization and new technologies are changing the ways that businesses communicate. We talk about "strategic" communication plans, about new "horizontal" and "collaborative" communication approaches, and theorize about "integrated" and "multichannel" models for disseminating information. All of this is of great interest to me as a communications professional, but it doesn't change the fact that in organizations of almost any size and complexity, information is still concentrated at the top. It resides in the narrow apex of C-suite offices, boardrooms, and conference rooms where knowledge is power, and vice versa. Whether we like it or not, the movement of critical information is inevitably *down*—from its fount at the top to the lowest rank and file.

For the moment, I'd like to focus on those at the bottom of the information pyramid—the rank and file, who usually know the least, but on whom the broad base of that pyramid rests and without whom the organization wouldn't exist.

We pay a lot of lip service to the "flow" of information. But sometimes it doesn't flow at all. Sometimes it's scarcely a trickle down. And all too often, those in power at the top work very hard to close the tap entirely.

How leaders communicate information to the workforce, how timely and how truthful that information is, is at the very heart of the issue of trust.

Information Brokering

Sometimes executives behave as information brokers, holding on to or hoarding information, based on their own agendas. Senior management employs a need-to-know-only basis for releasing information, but the need is often management's alone. Critical decisions about what employees might need to know are actually based on the goals, unvalidated assumptions, and even the secrets of those at the very top. And all too often, these decisions are made without genuine regard for the workforce.

The most common subject of information brokering surrounds compensation. Senior management is especially deceptive and evasive on the subject of finances. They don't want to talk to the rank and file about money. Executives don't want the workforce to know where the money goes. They don't want employees to know much money is available that could be paid out in compensation. Upon being told, "We can only do 1 percent raises this time," or "We can't do year-end bonuses," or "We're forced to pass on the increased cost of health insurance," employees may not openly question authority. But they know they're being denied vital information. And they've also received the message that the information brokers at the top of the pyramid just don't really care all that much about the fears, confusion, and suspicions of those down at the bottom.

I doubt that anything destroys trust faster in a corporate culture than evasive or defensive dialog from management about company finances. Yet leaders are often oblivious to the damage that this kind of information brokering can cause and amazed to discover that there may be another way.

Some years back we worked with a senior level executive who had become the CEO of a mid-cap microchip company headquartered in Silicon Valley. He had been appointed CEO on an interim basis because he was part of the VC group that had funded the company, but he was a banker by training, a CFO finance guy, now in the role of CEO of a high-tech company with hundreds of young Millennials in the workforce.

This new CEO, we'll call him John, contacted me when the company began making plans for their all-important annual meeting. The marketing department had come up with a "Speed of Sound" theme to emphasize the rapid growth that the company was experiencing. They wanted John to walk out on the stage in a flight suit, in front of a huge diorama showing F22 jets.

"I'm not walking out on a stage in a flight suit!" John told me. "They want me to talk about supersonic growth and acceleration of the business and all this stuff related to speed that's just over the top. I'm not comfortable with that. It's not who I am. It just doesn't sound like me."

"John," I said, "you're the CEO. The marketing department works for you, not the other way around. But what you need to do is to find out what the eight hundred people who are going to be in that room *want* you to talk about. It's not guesswork. Let's just ask them."

There wasn't much time, but we contacted about two dozen people, across all departments and all levels of employment, who were going to be in that audience. A clear consensus came back: they wanted their new CEO to address the current compensation structure.

Specifically, the employees were distressed over the structure of the new comp plan. Because of the way that the tiers and incentives had been set up, they were not making the money that they had been promised they would make, and they were pretty upset. When we presented this report to John, he wasn't pleased.

"I'm not talking about that either!" he said. "We have a compensation committee. We have a talent review committee. If the employees are unhappy about their pay, they need to follow proper channels. This isn't a subject for a CEO."

I knew I had to challenge him.

"John, the buck stops with you. This is the information issue that's going to be the stumbling block to your leadership. This is the elephant in the room. You can't pretend it's not there."

After much pulling and pushing, John agreed to address the issue head on. He still held to his conviction that "they just don't *understand* our finances," but he committed to exploring the complete compensation issue so that he could at least articulate it to the workforce.

After two days of internal meetings, however, what John discovered is that the employees had a good reason to be disgruntled. Given the marketplace and their new pricing strategy, the plan that had been created made it impossible for the company to meet incentive goals, resulting in as much as a 20 percent cut in compensation over the prior year. It would save the company money and increase profitability for the shareholders, but it wouldn't pay out what the employees had been led to expect.

In light of this discovery, and with John's permission, we came up with a whole new approach for the annual meeting and worked diligently with John on communicating directly, sincerely, and honestly. We got rid of all the staging, the sound track, the F22 fighter jets, and the expensive video, saving the company nearly 100K in staging fees. John walked out, in khakis and a golf shirt, onto an empty stage that displayed only a single visual on which was printed, "A Different Conversation." He stepped into a single spotlight at the front of the stage, looked out into the audience, and made eye contact with as many people as he could. After a long pause, he started his talk with the words, "I'm sorry."

He then delivered a short, straight talk about the misdirected compensation plan. The central message, which he repeated emphatically, was, "I am going to make this right." At the end of his talk, he received a long, enthusiastic, and completely genuine standing ovation. The company's next year was record-breaking, and to this day employees refer to John's "different conversation" speech and mark it as a turning point for the company.

In this case, John's own management was brokering information, masking reality with a message about supersonic growth. They were doing so in the mistaken belief that the workforce wouldn't be hurt by what they didn't know. John himself originally believed that the entire subject of employee pay was beneath his dignity, inappropriate for a CEO. There are other reasons, however, why leaders hoard information or hold off on telling the full truth. Like John's initial objections, they're not really reasons, they're excuses. They often hide deeper fears and leadership self-deceptions.

When the Truth Hurts

It shouldn't surprise us that leaders, being human, are hesitant to pass on bad news. The reluctance to communicate undesirable information is a widely documented phenomenon, first labeled the "Mum Effect" by Rosen and Tesser in 1970.[8] Their research, and many follow-up studies, suggests that this reluctance may be predicated on a fear of being infected with the emotional distress of the recipients. It's perfectly normal to want to avoid feeling the pain of others, particularly when we have some part in causing it. And it's all too easy for leaders at the top to avoid these messaging chores or to want to hand them off or down the chain of command.

I don't believe that's an option for authentic leadership. As John discovered, there's a tremendous trust benefit that accrues to leaders who are willing to step into that single spotlight of responsibility. And there's a cost to those who aren't. Leaders who refuse to look into the faces, and hearts, of the people affected by a crisis in their company risk seeing only the part of reality that serves them. They then get further out of touch with those they most need to reach.

Can you imagine BP's CEO Tony Hayward announcing, "I'd like my life back," while looking into the faces of those who had been affected by the Deepwater Horizon disaster? I certainly can't. But there's Hayward's statement, emblazoned forever on its special plaque in the Hall of Shame for the most out-of-touch CEOs.

Hayward's example is egregious. And crisis for most companies doesn't rise to the level of national ecological disaster. But many companies in the current economy are dealing with internal crisis and profound change. Their leaders are being evaluated by what they say and how they say it in times of crisis, and by the honesty and sensitivity with which they communicate bad news.

At Speakeasy, we're often called upon to help with high-stakes communications. Far too often, those stakes have become so high because some unpleasant truth has been avoided, postponed, or mishandled in the first place. Management has dug itself into a hole and made that hole deeper, creating a downward spiral of anxiety and distrust in their own workforce.

Let's face it. In the last couple of years, there's been a lot of bad news to communicate. As a result of the economic downturn and the recovery attempt, US businesses have been tasked with unprecedented demands for sending a variety of painful truths down the information pyramid. In the almost forty years that Speakeasy has been delivering executive coaching, our staff has run the full gamut of business and leadership issues, but never before have we faced with our clients the kind of demands they're facing for delivering messages that frankly don't come with an owner's manual.

Early in the economic meltdown we were asked to host a panel discussion for sixty members of the Atlanta Chamber of Commerce Board of Advisors Panel. The subject was "Crisis Communications" and the panelists were Speakeasy clients, all senior C-suite executives from three of Atlanta's well-positioned public companies. Coleman Breland, COO for Turner Broadcasting, Al Kabus, president of the Mohawk Group, and Tony Mitchell, CFO for Morrison Management Specialists, shared with us some of the trials of communicating bad news to external audiences and of delivering difficult messages to internal teams regarding layoffs and organizational changes.

Several of the panelists stressed the importance of technical preparation for layoffs and the benefit of getting the truth out quickly, rather than a trickle-down method that feeds prolonged distress and anxiety in the workforce. Some had even used sophisticated messaging matrixes to ensure that the right message was delivered to the right person and that each employee was personally thanked for specific service to the company. All emphasized that HR should be ready with help and information.

Not one of these successful leaders, however, proposed emails, phone calls, or form letters as acceptable methods of delivering bad news to employees. None suggested ways to shirk or delegate this responsibility of leadership, or even to economize on it. The common theme we heard, again and again, was the need for honesty and empathy. In the words of one panelist, the best approach is one that is "humble, gentle, and personal."

Many leaders have been faced with the painful challenge of communicating bad news in recent years. Here's Rick Robinson, senior vice president of Wells Fargo, describing how he met that challenge head on:

> Our firm recently went through a restructuring. I knew that rumors were rampant about what the restructure might look like and that obviously employees were concerned about their jobs. I called a team meeting to communicate the facts as I knew them. One of them, unfortunately, was that there would, indeed, be personnel reductions. I shared that the reductions would be based on criteria by which each individual would be

assessed. I answered every question put to me to the best of my ability. I closed by acknowledging the pain that would be felt by these displacements and that I knew the facts I'd shared couldn't make their concerns go away.

I know that the team appreciated receiving honesty rather than "spin" or corporate-speak about what was occurring. There was still uncertainty, but having the facts helped them not to dwell on what they couldn't control.

Sometimes the news is just bad and it hurts to tell it. But not being transparent on matters of strategy is counterproductive, particularly in times of change. Assuming that employees don't have the right to know, that they don't need to know, or somehow aren't capable of processing difficult information sells them, and the company, short.

When We Don't Have the Answers

The assumption is that leaders always know where they are going and how they're going to get there. Most of us weren't trained to like confusion or to admit when we feel hesitant and uncertain. In our schools and organizations, we place great value on sounding assured and confident and knowledgeable. Uncertainty has yet to emerge as a higher-order value or behavior that organizations eagerly reward.

The stereotype of the infallible executive persona and the deeply held belief that we must continually project an aura of confidence and competence makes it extraordinarily difficult for some leaders to just say, "I don't know." (For political leaders it seems nearly impossible.) It's much easier to throw up an obfuscating cloud of doublespeak, to offer a glib, condescending sound bite, or even to lie outright than to admit that we simply don't have the answer. But these are tactics that devalue both the question and the questioner. They may temporarily protect our image, but they are not ethical communications, and they don't engender trust.

> **It's better to know some of the questions than all of the answers.**
> **—James Thurber**

Even good leaders don't always have all the answers. And the great leaders aren't ashamed to admit it. Surprisingly, when leaders reveal uncertainty, and acknowledge that uncertainty with a little humility, the result is not less, but more respect and effort from the workforce. In the landmark five-year *Good to Great* study conducted by Jim Collins, personal humility was one of the most essential attributes of a great leader.[9] That's also the implication of a study led by Zakary Tormala of the Stanford University Graduate School of Business. "Expressing uncertainty, as opposed to utter confidence, draws people in," Tormala says.[10]

Leaders who already know everything, or try to give the impression that they do, are closed to growth, innovation, and change. They present themselves as unteachable and unreachable and fail to make authentic emotional connections. When leaders admit fallibility and reveal themselves as vulnerable, they engender a very human desire in employees to help that leader, and the company, find a way out of the quagmire. The quid pro quo is that employees usually work harder, with an energized spirit of cooperation.

When we drop the mask, stop trying to be the person we

think we're expected to be, and simply become the person we are, we open doors, making room for others and the solutions they may have.

When We Fear Distracting the Workforce

Perhaps the most baseless excuse I hear for withholding information is the fear of "distracting" the workforce. Particularly when companies are working on a divestiture, an acquisition, or a re-organization, this information will be withheld from employees in the belief that, should they learn of the organization's plans, they would become instant slackers, losing all initiative and motivation, except, of course, for looking for new jobs.

This is an insulting and paternalistic assumption that infantilizes employees and disregards their own needs and aspirations. It also overlooks the grapevine and the rumor mill that will fill the information vacuum anyway, probably with distorted information. It assumes that the workforce that is retained after a re-org or layoff will have no memory of how coworkers were treated or that the damage to trust won't have poisoned workplace culture.

My experience has been that companies who choose to communicate with full candor as much truth as they know, right when they know it, not only build trust in the workforce but find that employees continue to do their jobs. For an illustration of this, watch Michael Moore's documentary *Roger & Me* about the General Motors plant closings in Flint, Michigan.[11] I expect that, just as I was, you'll be moved by seeing these GM employees, even to the very last hour of their last day of employment, continuing to build cars with the same pride and diligence they had always brought to their work.

Uncertainty about how an initiative will go is a poor reason for information brokering. In the final analysis there just *aren't* any good reasons for keeping the workforce in the dark about material facts that affect their lives. Straight talk is always the best policy. In difficult times it may be the best retention strategy that organizations have.

As the economy begins to make slow progress back to recovery, organizations that have adopted a "you can't handle the truth" attitude with the workforce may discover the downside of information brokering pretty quickly. The most recent Deloitte Consulting LLP Ethics & Workplace Survey found that when the economy turns around, one-third (34 percent) of employed Americans plan to look for a new job. When asked what factors contributed to their plans to seek new work environments, 48 percent of employees cited a "loss of trust," and 46 percent said a "lack of transparency in communications."[12]

International studies echo Deloitte's data. The British CIPD Employee Outlook Survey for 2010 found that overall trust in leaders is low across the board, with only a third (34 percent) of employees agreeing that they trust their senior management teams and 38 percent disagreeing. Nearly half (47 percent) of employees who strongly distrust their senior management are currently looking for a new job compared to just 8 percent of workers who strongly trust their leaders.[13]

Claire McCartney, resourcing and talent advisor at CIPD, explained that trust is a key part of the employment relations that employers neglect at their peril: "If employees feel there is a gap between what directors say and do, or that there is a lack of transparency or fairness in terms of how people are recognized and rewarded, they are likely to feel disenchanted." McCartney pinpointed leadership communication that was frequent, open, and high quality as critical to earning and keeping workforce trust. [14]

I believe that most leaders genuinely value their workforce and want a trust relationship with their employees. But when we ask others to trust us, we assure them that they can rely on us to act on their behalf, to protect them when we can, and to take them into our confidences where their own welfare is concerned. In our most valuable relationships we have a moral duty of candor where truth and forthrightness is expected. We have an obligation to reveal what those who trust us ought to know for their own good, or want to know so that they can make informed decisions.

DARE!

Authentic leaders don't hide facts or sugarcoat realities just because they can. They dare to see their rank and file as partners, capable of understanding the complexities of the business, and entitled to the good news *and* the bad. When necessary, authentic leaders are strong enough to admit mistakes or acknowledge uncertainty, allowing others to see their human vulnerability, their willingness to accept help, and their openness to new ideas.

I dare you to think about what really motivates you. Ask yourself how important honest and straightforward information is to doing *your* best job. Recall how betrayed you've felt in the past when someone you trusted withheld critical information from you. If we aspire to a genuine trust relationship with our workforce, we must accept that our employees can handle the truth and have the right to know it. Our business is their business, too.

CHAPTER 5
NEW VALUES FOR GREAT LEADERS

The debate as to what makes a good leader has been going on a long time. It's not one very likely to be settled soon, either in the popular imagination or in the halls of academia. Over time, however, a number of different theories have been proposed, and the literature on leadership is interesting in revealing how our general ideas of great leadership have changed, or not.

In the early part of the twentieth century, the focus was on *trait* theories, which assumed that the capacity for leadership was inherent. Trait theorists took their cues from Thomas Carlyle's idea of the "Great Man"—a leader who was innately superior by virtue of extraordinary intelligence, courage, or other unique qualities that could capture the imagination of the masses. The Great Man's destiny was to rise to power when social conditions, or perhaps war, called for his talents, and he was often portrayed as mythic or heroic.

Trait theories fell out of favor, especially the Great Man view which was not only too sexist, but too elitist for more egalitarian times. The trait theories were largely supplanted by *behavioral* theories, which allowed for leadership development, and then by the *transactional* theories, first described by Max Weber in 1947. Transactional theories center on the ability of leaders to achieve organizational objectives by motivating employees through systems of reward and punishment. These theories are elegant, if mechanistic. There's no question that work is an economic exchange. No one, even today, is prepared to argue that standard forms of inducement, like promotions and pink slips, don't work. But observations of the success of more responsive, proactive leaders led to the concept of *transformational* leadership, defined by James MacGregor Burns in 1978, and expanded by Bernard M. Bass in 1985. Transformational theories focus on the connections formed between leaders and followers. These leaders seek to create intrinsic motivation by helping group members to see the importance and higher good of shared goals. Transformational leaders form emotional bonds with followers, inspiring them to transcend their own self-interest.

I'm not a proponent of trait theories, so I'm inclined to see some evolution in the shift to transactional theories, and even more progress in transformational theories with their emphasis on great leadership as the ability to create emotional connections with followers. Yet, if we conduct only a quick Google search, or pick up almost any of the many popular books on the subject today, we'll easily find lists of traits that are thought to be central to effective leadership. Books are still being written about "born leaders," and some of us apparently are even still looking for leadership genes. I recently discovered one book—and I'm not kidding about this—that proposes the "potential use of genetic information in creating job assignments and designing incentive and training plans."[15] What's even more interesting is the fact that, while decrying the Great Man theories, recent developments have shown us that the model is still alive and well. His unique qualifying characteristic is now called *charisma*.

The Charismatic Leader

In the last few decades, we've seen a rash of corporations bringing in high-profile, flamboyant CEOs in the hopes of motivating employees and instilling confidence in analysts and investors. The fame and force of personality of these celebrity CEOs does, indeed, capture the imagination of the masses and we reward them with superstar status. They ride in limousines and travel by private jet, surrounded by administrative staff, security teams, journalists, and often paparazzi. Their pictures appear on the covers of business publications, but also in popular, mainstream magazines. Some have significant political influence and are consulted by presidents and heads of state.

While many of these celebrity CEOs have unquestionable business talents, we tend to attribute all of the company's outcomes, including its performance, to the actions of its CEO. In the public perception the CEO *is* the company, getting credit through sheer force of personality for all of its success.

At least until something goes wrong. When the Great Man is discredited, when the stock tanks, scandal erupts, or the nightly news shows us our hero leaders in perp walks, then we revert to new-school thinking and demand to know why the "company" let this behavior go unchecked. How did so many drink the Kool-Aid? Here is Jim Collins, writing presciently in 1997, recognizing the attraction and the danger of the charismatic leader:

The old role is still seductive, though. Past models have glorified the individual leader, especially when he or she was an entrepreneur. And charismatic-style CEOs understandably find it hard to let go of the buzz that comes from having an intense, direct personal influence. But a charismatic leader is not an asset; it's a liability companies have to recover from. A company's long-term health requires a leader who can infuse the company with its own sense of purpose, instead of his or hers, and who can translate that purpose into action through mechanisms, not force of personality.[16]

I take a very slight exception to Collins's implication that charisma is always or necessarily bad, but I certainly follow, and wholeheartedly agree with, his larger point. Too many of the charismatic, celebrity CEOs that we've seen come and go recently have shown a conspicuous disregard for the future. Not just for the organization, its shareholders and employees, but for all of us who have been robbed of our faith and trust in corporate America. The implosion of Enron, Tyco, WaMu, World-Com, Smith Barney, Qwest, and the like should raise searching questions in all of us about the type of leadership that's worthy of admiration.

I don't believe that leadership can be reduced to, or described by, any single theory. At least not any I've run across yet. Beyond the will and desire to lead, I'm not sure there are any traits that are absolutely necessary for leaders. I've seen successful leaders who represent virtually every imaginable personality type and have emerged from every variety of educational, cultural, and economic background. My concern is for each person to find a way of leading that is congruent with who they really are. To do this we first need to know our own core values and beliefs, be able to communicate them to others, and then ensure that our actions always match our words. This is authentic leadership. It's much more about where a leader stands than where he or she is going. It's the important constant in the face of changing business strategies and changing economic climates. It's the steadiness of presence that inspires others and infuses corporate culture with a clear sense of principle and vision that will stand the test of time.

 In matters of style, swim with the current. In matters of principle, stand like a rock.
—Thomas Jefferson

As for charisma? Maybe I have a different definition. But I've found that charisma naturally emanates from those whose values and behavior are coherent and consistent, even if it's a less flamboyant, less narcissistic, kind of magnetism.

Rather than succumbing to a cult of personality or focusing on leadership traits and styles, it seems time instead to think about *values*. Values that can be put into action as pathways to self-discovery for achieving the congruency that informs authentic leadership.

The Self-Aware Leader

There's a lot of overlap in the thousands of books, hundreds of websites, and scores of articles and papers that offer up lists of the most important skills of successful leaders. Few of them include what may be the least acknowledged leadership competency: a high level of self-awareness. And yet, self-awareness forms the very foundation of many of the skills that these lists promote. It's the cornerstone of the social competence on which transformational leadership depends and the basis of the emotional intelligence that theorists like Daniel Goldman have found to be twice as important as IQ, technical skills, or analytical reasoning for highly effective leadership.[17]

A low level of self-awareness accounts for the poor interpersonal skills that make it hard for leaders to connect to others and all but precludes transformational leadership. But a lack of self-awareness also prevents us from really knowing our own values and priorities, making us susceptible to ethical fading and the temptations of money and power that have brought down so many in the last decade. It blocks us from acknowledging our own weaknesses and thus impedes the skill development that we may desperately need. At the same time, it also keeps us from discovering our strengths and passions—the gifts that allow us to thrive in our work. Leaders with low levels of self-awareness are effectively blind, to their own emotions and drives as well as to their effect on others. To use the analogy of Gestalt psychologist Fritz Perls, "They live in a house of mirrors and think they're looking out."

The flip side of self-awareness is self-delusion, which is precisely why the path to self-awareness is so challenging. We simply don't know that we don't know. Unfortunately, for many individuals, self-discovery never happens. For others, when it does, it often coincides with an existential crisis. The spouse who we didn't know was unhappy suddenly asks for a divorce. A friend suddenly and inexplicably distances herself. The company that we believe we are serving well passes us over for promotion or decides to let us go. Some other event may shock us into the realization that others perceive us quite differently from the way we perceive ourselves. We learn, abruptly, that we are not at all the person we thought we were. In my own case, it was that epiphany, eighteen years ago, when I learned that the Scott Weiss I thought I was projecting was not the one being received, and the one being received was not one I liked. Events like these have started many people on the path to self- awareness, but it needn't take a crisis.

Self-awareness is certainly not a personality trait. It's not a cognitive skill like analytical reasoning. It's not an innate talent, but rather a capability subject to learning and thus within reach for all of us. It's the deep process of discovery and exploration of how people experience us as human beings. In theory, it should be the life-work of all of us, but for leaders who are charged with guiding others, it may be the single foundational competency most worthy of attention and development.

Ron Ricci, who is the vice president of corporate positioning at Cisco, is one of those leaders who has made a life work of self-discovery. He recently shared with me a story about one of those times when that work really paid off.

> It was the company's annual leadership conference. I was on the stage, about to deliver a prepared speech to two thousand Cisco leaders, when the electricity failed. Now, it's one thing to deliver a rehearsed presentation in front of so many people. It's quite another to find yourself in a completely spontaneous situation with your boss looking up at you from his seat in the audience and thousands of your peers wondering how you are going to handle the crisis.
>
> I'm lucky enough to have had communication training

and self-assessments that have revealed my bias as an introvert. Because I'm self-aware of my introverted nature, I completely understood what was happening to me on that dark stage and knew the reasonable thing for an introvert to do. I needed to shift the attention away from myself and point the non-existent spotlight to something or someone else. In this case, there was no better extrovert to invite on stage than the CEO of Cisco, John Chambers.

Miraculously, at about the same time, the microphones started working again. The stage and the projectors were still dark, but John was up on the stage with me. Perhaps it was my introverted nature, but I assumed that once he got on stage he would, well, just take over. The exact opposite happened. He decided that his best way to handle the crisis was, heaven forbid, to talk with me on the stage. He turned to me and asked me why it was that Cisco had been able to build a culture around collaboration, instead of competing with one another.

I wasn't prepared for that, either, and, as an introvert, I couldn't stand being the center of attention, but this was my job after all. So I just blurted out, "I really appreciate your giving me a one-on-one review of my job performance in front of two thousand of my peers."

The line got laughs, but I didn't say it for laughs. The introvert in me was simply trying to avoid the attention. But John didn't let me off the hook. He just stood there, looking at me. This was turning into a career moment and I suddenly knew it. I needed to trust my instincts with what I said next. I needed to be smart and answer the question.

I decided to believe in what I've learned about myself. I'm a conceptual thinker, a dot connector who is attracted to ideas. I was connecting dots over this three- or four-second interval. Some people like to build a story and lead up to an answer. I've discovered I'm not like that. I like to start with the answer, an anchor idea, or thought. Only one word emerged in my head: *Trust.* So I said it. "Trust is what makes Cisco's culture of teamwork and collaboration work."

What came next was actually easy. I went on to describe how I believed that one of Cisco's most significant areas of collaboration innovation was the simple common vocabulary that Cisco uses to make decisions, and how this vocabulary had eliminated much of the ambiguity in decision-making that trips up so many leaders. When I think back on this experience, I realize how important it was for me to know myself. All my personality characteristics were at work in just a few minutes time.

Genuine Feedback

The first step to self-awareness is the willingness to listen to those around you. That means actively soliciting feedback from others, working to constantly improve that feedback, and continually communicating and demonstrating that it will be used constructively. Ironically, however, by the time that many leaders reach the C-suite—when they have the greatest influence over others and the greatest need for self-awareness to guide their decisions—they have also become exempt from any genuine feedback process. Other than from the oversight of a board of directors or a very senior boss, opinions about their personality and behavior only come through in responses to formal presentations, secondhand reports, or perhaps the observations of business journalists. This exemption from feedback is unfortunate and reinforces the assumption that leaders at the top are somehow "finished" and beyond all need for self-development. The case is very much otherwise.

! **Feedback is the breakfast of champions.**
—Ken Blanchard

Leaders need to know how they are being received by coworkers, customers, management teams, and the rank and file they lead. Obviously, the higher we are in the organization the more difficult it will be to get honest, objective feedback. Leaders who are really serious about coming out of their house of mirrors will find a way to get anonymous feedback from staff members and coworkers. We need to actively and repeatedly demonstrate that the messenger won't get shot and consistently create opportunities for others to raise concerns. Inserting a step during important decision-making processes where contrariness is encouraged and honesty is nurtured can be of personal as well as organizational benefit. Assigning a devil's advocate in meetings and discussions can help to insure that ideas and proposals receive a thorough critique and risk analysis. Feedback through any mechanism is really a gift, even if it's one we must sometimes ask to be given.

Advisors and Counselors

While many executives are assiduous about maintaining their financial, and even physical, health, the notion of going to a psychological "gym" to improve mental fitness for leadership, and for life, seems absurd. The stereotype of the strong, competent leader who has all the answers and never admits to self-doubt or self-questioning precludes our seeking help from professional counselors. It's a sad commentary on our societal values that reaching out for such help should carry a stigma. Even the U.S. military has difficulty getting veterans, combat-hardened in Iraq and Afghanistan, to ask for or to accept counseling. But the decision to seek help from trained professionals is not only an act of courage, it can be a fast track to heightened self-awareness. Psychometric testing and personality assessments like the Myers-Briggs and the Birkman Method tools can also yield some valuable surprises in how you relate to specific others and to the world at large. When the need arises, an expert point of view—for those who are strong enough to reach out for it—can foster the deeper understanding that self-learning brings about.

Coaching and Mentoring

As you begin to discover the gap between the current reality and the one you desire, you may want to consider a coach or mentor. Learning from the accumulated wisdom of elders, tribal matriarchs, chieftains, or shamans is the oldest type of knowledge transfer known to man, and modern-day versions still work. Research has repeatedly shown the pay-off for coaching and mentoring, not just in better performance, but also in increased job satisfaction, decreased turnover, and rewards that spill over into the personal sphere. In the humility required to open oneself to guidance and the quiet centering that is necessary for listening and learning, we can glean many benefits. Those fortunate enough to have the opportunity and to take advantage of a coaching or mentoring relationship are usually enriched on many dimensions.

I have sought out many mentors in my life. Sandy Linver

was a very important one in the early years with Speakeasy that had a profound impact on my life. But even while I was working with Sandy over ten years, I also had other mentors advising me. Working one-on-one with someone you trust and who will assess you honestly can bring about great leaps in self-awareness and personal growth.

A Network of Credible Voices

Finally, leaders who are committed to the quest for self-awareness will work to create and surround themselves with what I call "a network of credible voices." These should be people who are not on your payroll, who have no skin in the game that would prevent them from giving you accurate assessments of your current reality. Solicit personal feedback and counseling from individuals who can provide informed, fine-grained advice on not only the leadership capacities that you already exhibit but those that require better development. It is hard to correct what we don't know we're not doing. These trusted voices can help us track how we're evolving in our ongoing quest for self-awareness. They can keep the dialog open and hold up a more accurate mirror for us in revealing how others see us in a variety of important situations. The literature on leadership is filled with examples of those who refused to ask for advice from others, but the history books show us that the wisest leaders have always sought broad counsel. Behind every great leader you'll probably find one or more trusted advisors who act as sage counselors and discreet sounding boards.

We can make huge gains in self-awareness by finding out what others know about us that we don't, but we've still got to process that information. We need the time and space to focus on our strengths and weaknesses, our drives and personalities, our habits and values. In short, we need time to *think* about our process of becoming and what we feel. This is why I would rank self-reflection and introspection as inestimable leadership values.

Self-Reflection

We bemoan it all the time, even as we're madly punching away with our thumbs into our BlackBerries and iPhones. The technologies that have allowed us to be more productive now threaten to enslave us. They're actually creating more demands on our time and attention, encroaching on spaces previously reserved for family, for introspection, for rest, or simply for doing nothing. In our "always wired, always on" world, we're rapidly changing the dynamics of how we operate and interact, becoming conditioned to constant interruption, scattered thinking, and hyperactivity. We call this "multi-tasking" and perversely take pride in it, equating our busyness with how important we are and how valuable we are. I think we're kidding ourselves, and the neuroscience backs me up.

The truth is that the human brain is incapable of actually focusing on two things at the same time. What we're actually doing is simply switching tasks, hopping between them very rapidly, but also with swift shifts in attention and corresponding drops in performance. When we talk on the phone while typing an email, we may think we're multitasking. Neuroscientists like Earl Miller say we need to think again. "You cannot focus on one while doing the other," says Miller. "That's because of what's called interference between the two tasks. They both involve communicating via speech or the written word, and so there's a lot of conflict between the two of them."[18]

When that conflict gets us into trouble, and we accomplish any of those tasks poorly, we claim that we "didn't have time" or blame the technology, deflecting responsibility for the emails rife with spelling and grammatical errors, the critical information we omitted, the generally distorted communication, or the bad, split-second decisions made on the fly.

Multitasking is a human delusion. It's thus an absurd competency to hire for and to reward in our employees, and an even more absurd skill for leaders to esteem. Yet this standard of constant hyperactivity is becoming the new norm. We not only think we must be doing *something* all the time, but *many* things at the same time. We text while we eat, talk while we drive, compose emails while watching TV, and don't even blink at the oxymoronic concept of the "working vacation."

In the often breakneck pace of today's workplace, we put a lot of emphasis on this imagined ability to do many things at once. We especially esteem leaders who can react to fast changes and make quick decisions on behalf of the organization. The ability to think "on one's feet," as they say, may sometimes be necessary. But it's probably not the best posture for producing decisions that have far-reaching or long-term consequences. And those who do it well, seemingly intuitively, are often those doing a lot of homework in the background. These are leaders who have already developed the habit of putting aside time to reflect not only on current decisions but past mistakes and lessons learned.

I often hear executives say, "I'm pressed for time." I rarely hear one say, "That deserves consideration. I'm going to have to take some time to think about that." Yet thoughtful decision-making usually leads to better results and most of history's great leaders have known this. Abraham Lincoln is only one example of the many great leaders who understood the value of stealing away for self-reflection. Lincoln frequently removed himself from the White House to a cottage at the Soldier's Home to consider the implications of his decisions. It was there that he learned the results of Gettysburg and wrote the Emancipation Proclamation.

 For every five well-adjusted and smoothly functioning Americans, there are two who never had the chance to discover themselves. It may well be because they have never been alone with themselves.
—Marya Mannes

More subdued, introverted leaders will not need much convincing of the need to carve out space for self-reflection and introspection. It's the exceptionally outgoing, charismatic leader who especially needs to get away from his or her own press, to shut out the clamor, and quiet the body and mind. Taking time for reflection may not come easy for these individuals. If you're uncomfortable at first with the silence, with the lack of distraction or tasks to do, this should tell you something. It's easy to confuse "busyness" with business. But we all know that they're not equivalent. A daily scheduled time for thoughtful reflection on where you are, who you are, and what your leadership means to those you influence should be at least as important as a coffee break, answering emails, or returning a phone call. The excuse that we don't have time to honor and calendar our need for quiet contemplation amounts to an admission that we're willing to accept the idea that we don't need it to make good decisions.

My own personal journey, and what I've witnessed in the journeys of others, has convinced me that it's all but impossible to understand how to connect authentically with others without first connecting with oneself. We can't guide others until we know what guides ourselves. Without first clarifying our own essential values, beliefs, and intentions, it seems impossible to communicate a vision that others can share. We won't exhibit the consistency that makes others see clearly what we stand for, trust us, and want to share in the sense of purpose out of which collective action grows.

Vulnerability

We equate the very word "vulnerability" with weakness and the susceptibility to being wounded or hurt. We certainly don't think of vulnerability as a typical leadership value. You won't often find it as the subject of management workshops or leadership development courses. But the truth is that we're all vulnerable, because we're all human. Pretending otherwise, covering up, attacking when a soft spot gets touched—techniques that each of us have used at one time or another—are really pure poses, and over time these defenses become not only draining, but deadening.

Acknowledging vulnerability is not about looking weak. It's about allowing yourself to be exposed to your own emotions and the emotions of others. Identifying with the frustration in customer complaints, empathizing with the disappointments or personal losses of team members, or simply sharing how you really feel in the moment are evidences of our basic humanity. Human beings who don't feel for anyone beyond themselves are infants. Usually they outgrow this infantile state, coming to recognize that others also experience pain and joy and learning to share in the emotional dimensions of communication. Those who don't outgrow this state, or can't, we call *sociopaths*, or more kindly, *narcissists*, but we acknowledge pathology in their emotional limitations. It's strange, then, that the notion of being emotionally vulnerable should have acquired such negative connotations. As leaders we need reminding that the ability to feel, and to feel deeply, is not a weakness, but the hallmark of a fully mature individual.

 Never apologize for showing emotion. When you do so, you apologize for the truth.
—Benjamin Disraeli

We talk a lot these days about "thought" leaders. I wish we talked more about "feeling" leaders, not to minimize the thinking process, but to place more emphasis on the feeling that accompanies the thinking. By themselves, thoughts are static things. The most brilliant idea in the world just lies there, in the mind of its creator, until it's coupled with emotion. Emotions are the fuel for behavioral change. They ignite our thoughts, transforming the way we act and speak, putting the power into our persuasion, the energy into our mission, and the passion into our work. Understanding our own emotions is essential if we're going to elicit emotional responses in others, who also need this fuel to catch fire.

Rather than being embarrassed by them, great leaders are highly conscious of their own emotions and empathetic to the feelings of others. Emotions are not obstacles, but critical elements of their success. Our own vulnerability is our most valuable human asset.

In my own experience in working with leaders, I've repeatedly witnessed that when they are confident enough to show their basic human vulnerability, they create tighter, more trusting teams. When they are able to share personal stories of deeply trying challenges or times when they experienced doubt or confusion, great joy, or personal growth, they create strong personal bonds with those they lead. Occasionally, abandoning the confidence-based rhetoric to reveal vulnerability is risky. But it can reap great rewards for leaders and their teams. David Kohl, who is executive vice president of Vevo, recently shared with me his own experience of a time when he took that risk. Here's David's story:

> About two years ago, I was preparing to deliver the year-end wrap for my entire team and for the offices that would be calling in. We were about to head into the holiday break and I really wanted to inspire them for the coming year, but I was thinking about a couple of individuals who had come to me in the last months to express doubts about what they were doing. They were questioning their careers and the value of their work and what was really important to them. They were working really, really hard, but they had begun to have doubts about why they were doing it.
>
> My response to them had been, "Think about it!" Don't get caught on this wheel and keep doing what you're doing if you're really not happy. We have an amazing company, and amazing people, and we're having a lot of fun. But if in your heart of hearts you know this isn't what you should be doing, that's OK. If you want to make a switch, I'll help you transition to something you're passionate about. If you're not passionate about this, then maybe you shouldn't be here. Because when you're passionate about something, you know it's the right thing and you're psyched to do it every day.
>
> I had just finished reading the book *The Alchemist* to my

son and my thoughts kept returning to that experience. The book is about finding your own personal destiny. It's about taking a hard look at your life and learning to trust the omens or intuitive signs that jump out of your inner being and will guide you to the right place if you pay attention to them.

I decided to take a risk and depart from the usual end-of-the-year business cheerleading speech. I gave a copy of the book to everyone in the room and began telling them instead about the special experience that *The Alchemist* had allowed my son and me to share. At the end of the book my son had started speaking to me about his own intuition, about some of the things he wanted to do. He told me that he had decided that he wanted a life connected to the arts and music, but also to science and nature. I knew about the music, of course, but I had never heard about the science and I was moved that he felt his own inner signs guiding him in that direction. It had been such a warm, revealing moment that it had literally brought me to tears. When I told the story in the meeting, I was moved to tears again. So were other people in that room.

When everyone came back after the holidays it seemed clear that we had made a deeper connection and a stronger bond. Many people reached out to tell me how much they appreciated the book and the story I'd shared. They told me that it had given them a renewed passion and dedication to the work they were doing. There was great feedback from the outer offices, too, where many had also bought and read the book.

As it turned out, there were also individuals who took the message to heart to make a change. A gentleman who was my VP on the West Coast wanted to do something more entrepreneurial. An account manager also resigned. He had decided that he wanted to be a doctor. We figured out a transitional plan for him to work until he was accepted into med school. Obviously I hated to lose these people, but I'm confident that they made the right decisions for them.

I think that the risk David took in sharing his personal experience and that little book with his team was rewarding for everyone involved. His example shows how embracing our vulnerability can make us more effective and authentic leaders.

Honesty and Transparency

I've already focused on transparency as it pertains to information brokering and customer relationships, but it's a drum I'm going to keep beating because of its centrality to the creation of trust. The events of the last years and the global trust fall have made a powerful case for the need for transparency within organizations, but it's the job of leaders to model that transparency. As Gandhi said, "You must be the change you wish to see in the world."

As a human value, transparency is akin to what we call "perfect" honesty, or honesty that goes beyond the call of duty. At those times when someone begins a statement with, "Well, to be *perfectly* honest," the information that follows is likely to be more than a mere transference of objective facts. What follows may be a subjective, emotion-laden revelation: *"To be perfectly honest, I'm terrified of public speaking and don't want to deliver that talk."* It may contain criticism, offered in a spirit of helpfulness: *"To be perfectly honest, I thought you were a bit condescending with Jones and didn't give his idea a fair hearing."* It may simply reveal the speaker's own doubt or vulnerability: *"To be perfectly honest, I'm worried about this plan and think we may be on the wrong track."*

The differences between simple honesty and real transparency are subtle but significant. When our doctor tells us that we're forty pounds overweight, she's being honest. When she tells us that, unless we immediately and radically change our lifestyle and diet, she foresees our early death, she's being transparent. Brutally so, we might feel at the moment. But with only a little reflection, we recognize that the stretch to perfect honesty has been for our own good.

Erika Andersen, the founder of Proteus International, Inc., and a well-known executive coach, is familiar with the difference that the push to genuine honesty and transparency can mean. Erika recently shared this story:

> A few years ago, I was talking with a CEO I coach about a big meeting he was going to be conducting in a few weeks. We were going over the agenda together in preparation, since I was going to be facilitating it for him. They were selling a part of their business, and most people felt unsettled and uncomfortable about it. People weren't sure it was a good idea, and it was going to involve a pretty significant layoff as well. He and I were talking about how to conduct that part of the meeting, and whether to invite Q&A.
>
> Suddenly he said, "You know, we don't need to talk about this. Everybody's tired of hearing about it."
>
> I could have just agreed and moved on. He was, after all, the client. It was his meeting. But I was pretty sure people *really* wanted to hear about it. They were the senior staff and wanted all the available information.

I put down the page and said, "You want me to be perfectly honest with you, right?"

He frowned, but nodded. I looked right into his eyes.

"I think people are hungry to know what's actually going on. I think this is more about your discomfort with the topic than their not wanting to talk about it."

He didn't say anything for a minute; just looked down at his copy of the agenda and tapped his pen against it. I had a moment to wonder if I'd been more honest than he was able to hear.

Finally, he looked up. "OK, damn it, you're right," he said. Then he actually smiled. "Glad somebody calls me on my crap."

I left his office feeling great, knowing I'd taken a risk that had paid off for both of us.

* * *

As leaders, we're confronted nearly every day with situations in which we must choose to lie, to be honest, or to be honest without being fully transparent—to stop just shy of a truth that might foster growth and change. My colleague, peer, or subordinate asks for an assessment and I must choose between a kind and merely honest response or a more transparent one that isolates areas for improvement or sheds light on a blind spot. I enter a meeting with the Board to update them on the business and have to choose, again, between honesty and transparency. Do I share with them what they want to hear, or do I share with them what's really going on? That I'm nervous about the economy, scared that our new initiative might fail, worried because there's a new competitor gaining market share? If I were truly transparent,

I would let them "see inside" my mind and hear what's really going through it. My transparency is optional. But the difference it might make to the Board's decisions and the future of the organization is critical.

Transparency is closely tied to vulnerability. Some people are just naturally more transparent than others. They're more grounded and more confident with who they are, and just don't see transparency as a risk. The win is that teams are motivated by transparent people because those leaders can be trusted. Everyone has the ability to be more transparent, but it requires accepting that personal risk. You have to put yourself out there.

These values, and the behaviors that manifest from them, may not be forceful or flashy or showy. They may not produce "charisma" in the popular sense of the word. But they will certainly produce more personally mature individuals, more authentic leaders, and more high-trust organizations for now and the future.

DARE!

Great leaders make the quest for self-awareness a lifelong project. They commit to rooting out self-deception and seek a more genuine understanding of the impact of their thoughts, feelings, and behavior on others. I dare you to find and encourage all of the feedback mechanisms available to you in your personal life and in the organization and turn them into open and safe dialogs where you can learn from others. I dare you to consider professional counseling, coaching, or mentoring to support your change efforts and to work to create a network of credible voices who will be willing resources to monitor your own reality checks.

Self-Reflection

Wise leaders honor their own need for quiet self-reflection. They respect thoughtful, considerate decision-making over multitasking in themselves and their employees. I dare you to calendar and honor at least one hour a day of uninterrupted time for self-reflection on your roles as a leader.

Vulnerability

It takes courage to be vulnerable, but great leaders take the risk. They know that their emotions are among their greatest leadership strengths and the means of connecting most authentically and powerfully with those they lead. Do you dare to become more open to how you really feel? Can you accept the risk of allowing others to see who you really are?

Honesty and Transparency

Great leaders are not only honest, but they know that transparency is a human value as well as an organizational one. We have a responsibility to be "perfectly honest" when the welfare of others is at stake. I dare you to embrace and to model transparency as a core leadership value.

CHAPTER 6
CUSTOMER CONVERSATIONS

Once upon a time—in the living memory of many of us—the concept of good customer service was a fairly straightforward notion. You offered a good product or service to a willing and trusting buyer. In all likelihood the transaction was completed face-to-face, with a smile, a handshake, and a sincerely delivered "thank you." The next time you saw your customer you remembered him or her, and perhaps asked about the family. At any time that something went wrong after a sale, you apologized and quickly made it right. You valued the relationship more than any single sale.

That "old" way of doing business is becoming more and more rare. Today the customer is increasingly faceless and anonymous, the customer relationship increasingly digitized. Even the most traditional types of businesses now have become "brick and click," and the e-commerce trend isn't slowing down. Forrester projects online sales to rise to $278 billion by

2015, a 9.62 percent compound annual growth rate for the three-year forecast period.[19]

Yet the growth of the internet, advances in technology, and the globalization of the marketplace mean more customers to serve and more ways to serve them. In the last decade, whole industries have sprung up built around the idea of maximizing the customer experience at all "points of contact," from traditional media to website interaction, social media management, help centers, and more. Correspondingly, but not coincidentally, there has also arisen another entire set of new industries wholly devoted to defending consumers against poor customer service. These take many forms, including consumer-activist websites hosted by non-profits, product review spaces where disgruntled consumers tell tales and name names, blogs and columns devoted to frauds and scams, and even featured segments on local evening newscasts. In my own city, Atlanta, consumer advocate Clark Howard hosts a daily talk show partially devoted to "Customer No-Service."

It would appear that managing customer relationships has become exponentially complex, as well as expensive, and that the goal of creating customer loyalty is both challenging and mysterious. A lot has changed, we think. But has it really?

I'm convinced that it hasn't. I believe that the principles for building trust with customers in the digital age are exactly the same as they have always been for building trust between human beings. Doing business with machines doesn't make me one. And however much I'm compelled to deal with faceless corporate automatons, or their software, I'd much prefer to buy from *people*. I like my transactions to include a little of the human touch and still expect my commercial conversations to resemble human ones. While I may be a fan of your product or service, genuine satisfaction and enduring loyalty come from another source. They're generated by the way you treat me and talk to me.

The Emotional Connection

At Speakeasy we sometimes have difficulty convincing our executive clients that it's okay to show a little emotion. Invariably, when they do, and when that emotion is sincere and appropriate, they make stronger connections with their audiences and peers. The ability to "hear" and to empathize with one another's feelings is critical to human bonding. It shouldn't surprise us then that, even in the Internet Age, it's also critical to customer satisfaction.

One of these newer customer relationship consulting companies, Beyond Philosophy, recently interviewed fifty-three customer experience executives as part of its 2011 Global Customer Experience Management Survey. Some of their results were unexpected and even seem counterintuitive. One finding was that it's not about the money; investing more resources in a better customer experience doesn't necessarily result in happier customers. Some of the companies with the worst survey results—companies like Hewlett-Packard and HSBC—are among those spending the most on customer experiences.[20]

Instead, it seems that emotions "account for more than half the typical customer experience," according to the survey. And people's feelings about a company often depend on the company's ability to gauge customer emotions. It turns out that technology companies, including Apple, are especially good at understanding customer emotions. The iPhone maker also recently came out on top in the American Customer Satisfaction Index and in J.D. Power's Smartphone Customer Satisfaction Survey.

In the eight years that Apple has been leading the PC industry in customer satisfaction, its stock price has increased by 2,300 percent.[21] While there's no doubt that the company's innovative products account for much of that connection, Apple fans are well known for being not merely emotional, but often rabidly passionate about the brand. The Apple experience is a highly emotional one.

All businesses would like to have the kind of customers that Apple has acquired. We'd like to convert satisfied customers to loyal customers and loyal customers to raving fans who will buy more and more frequently and will tell their friends about our products and services. Yet we don't seem to make the emotional connections with our customers that inspire that kind of loyalty.

 They may not remember what you say, but they'll definitely remember how you made them feel.

Instinctually we realize, from our own personal experiences as a consumer, that customers are highly influenced by their emotional experiences with a brand. Yet we still approach customer acquisition and retention as though it were a purely rational process and cling to the notion that we only need better, more logical arguments to convince people of our point of view. In business school, we're taught that the costs of obtaining a new customer are very high, and that the profitability of a loyal customer grows with the relationship's duration. Yet we still think of customer service as a "cost center"—a division that piles up expenses without bringing in revenue.

Within many businesses there's still a profound lack of clarity on how customer loyalty happens, and a dangerous naiveté in the idea that we can simply market our way into our customer's hearts.

Faking Sincerity

"The secret of success," said the French playwright Jean Giraudoux, "is sincerity. Once you can fake that, you've got it made." It's a funny line. Or it would be if so many of us weren't subjected to canned spiels, false friendliness, and orchestrated insincerity every day of our lives.

"Your call is important to us," says the prerecorded voice while we wait on hold, number thirty-seven in the queue, knowing that when we eventually connect with a person we're likely to be relayed a few more times, re-entering the queue, starting over each time with our complaint and account number. From "Welcome to X-mart" to "Have a nice day," scripted insincerities, of the second-hand-car-salesman type, pervade nearly every area of modern commerce. We've become so accustomed to the flow of prepared spiels and empty platitudes that we rarely bother to take offense. It's a function of modern life, we think.

And yet every single one of us has actually *had* an exceptional customer experience. We all recall a time that someone actually heard us, related to us as an individual, and went out of their way to help or give us information that didn't come from a sales spiel or script. These are experiences that transcend the "rational" physical attributes like quality, quantity, delivery, and even price.

At the end of a recent stay at a W Hotel in San Francisco, I dropped by the front desk to complain about not finding the expected copy of *USA Today* outside my room's door. The front desk manager informed me that the policy of providing the newspapers had been discontinued because the hotel chain was "going green." I was a little suspicious of his explanation and decided to file a grievance with the chain's headquarters. I expected, eventually, to receive an automated email acknowledging my complaint, but I generally forgot about the incident.

Imagine my surprise a few days later when an area vice president for Starwood Properties in San Francisco called my Atlanta office to apologize. And not in a way I expected. He was sorry, he said, that I had been misinformed (read: lied to) by the desk manager. The truthful reason that they had stopped distributing the papers was an effort to increase profit margins since they didn't believe it would affect the customers' stay. I was deeply impressed, not just by the personal contact from this executive, but with his astonishingly refreshing honesty. I'll stay at the W again. Even without the newspaper.

I'll buy again, too, from my local drugstore where the pharmacist remembers me and always suggests the less expensive generic alternative. I'm loyal to my auto mechanic who doesn't fix it if it isn't broken and tells me the truth when he can't find the problem. I drive far out of my way to eat at the modest little restaurant that always treats my family like VIPs. I'm delighted by L.L. Bean's and Nordstrom's no-questions-asked return policies. Even in more impersonal interactions with call centers and online commerce, I react to the human touches. I'm happily surprised when I call anybody these days and am greeted by a human voice. I feel appreciated when Direct TV thanks me for being a customer since 1993.

There are no traffic jams along the extra mile.
—Roger Staubach

Some customer experiences are just memorable. We tell others about them, becoming evangelists for the product or service or store. We relay these experiences personally, at lunch, at the water cooler, or over the phone, but increasingly to the two billion other customers now online. In addition to the multitude of customer service horror stories that fill internet review sites and social media, there are a lot of positive stories, too. Stories in which customers are excitedly telling others about an experience that generated not just satisfaction, but genuine emotions. Feelings of gratitude, passion, and dare I say it? Even love.

For companies that sincerely value their customers, "Have a nice day" just doesn't cut it. Some are willing to dig a little deeper, talk a little straighter, and engage in authentically human ways. And some are even managing to do this in the vast, impersonal digital universe.

Last year's winner of the National Retail Federation's Customer Choice Award (and a top-ten winner since 2007), online shoe retailer Zappos has used a loyalty-based business model from the beginning, creating a culture around the brand that naturally encourages repeat buying. Amazon bought the company in 2009, but Zappos was allowed to keep its independent entity and branding. It has also kept its loyal consumer base.

At Zappos, a 342-person, round-the-clock customer loyalty team answers 5,000 calls a day, 1,200 emails a week, and monitors Twitter and social networking sites for mentions of Zappos, which they use to proactively reach out to potential shoppers.

Zappos operators don't have quotas or call-time limits. They don't read from scripts. They use their real names. Zappos views the phone experience as a branding device, and speaks to virtually every customer at least once.

When asked in an *Adweek* interview why the Zappos approach has resonated so well, CEO Tony Hsieh had this to say:

> I think part of it is we're very transparent. One of our core values is being open and honest. It ends up creating more trust with our customers, employees, and partners. It's the opposite of what most businesses do. Most try to be secret with their secret strategies."[22]

There is much that is inspiring about the Zappos approach to serving customers, but I think Tony Hsieh hit the nail on the head about secrecy. Like most of us, I'm frequently frustrated by the lengths to which some businesses go to make the customer experience so darn difficult. From eliminating or burying the customer service number in advertisements and web pages to obscuring forms, terms, and conditions with impossible language and illegible text; from creating content that customers can't read to hiding extra fees to throwing up layers of bureaucracy that distance customers from those with the real knowledge and ability to solve their problems.

Does it really make sense to treat our customers this way? To deliberately distance ourselves from them, waste their time, even insult their intelligence down to the level of language? The value of euphemism, by the way, has been in a significant downward spiral since the day that used cars became "pre-owned." Do we actually feel more welcome at the superstore that calls us a "guest" rather than a customer? Does it save us any money when charges for annual dues suddenly become an "investment"? Does anyone still believe that the bank's "privacy" policy messaging, delivered in legalese and microscopic print, really relates to *our* privacy? How many people are left on earth who don't yet know that a "customer loyalty award" is a bribe, or who still hold to the fantasy of the "free gift"?

Not many. Customers are seeing through this baloney and getting tired of secret strategies. If we really wanted to serve our customers well, we wouldn't work to mask our actions. We would talk to them in the language they use, not in slogans or adspeak. Our customer conversations are either honest and genuine or they're not. Our words align with our actions or they don't. We can be phony and manipulative, secretive and insincere, demonstrating that we value the customer's dollar, but not really the customer. Or we can borrow what we know from our personal relationships and make emotional connections through the same dynamics that create trusting friendships. By telling the truth, we reveal what's important and demonstrate that we care more about the relationship than the transaction.

Transparency Not Optional

Ideally, all leaders should want to set the example of demanding candor and transparency in customer interactions. But the truth is that the internet is leaving them little choice. In today's world, where information travels globally at the speed of a mouse click, transparency is no longer simply desirable, it is becoming unavoidable.

The Ethisphere Institute is a leading international think-tank dedicated to the creation, advancement, and sharing of best practices in business ethics, corporate social responsibility, anti-corruption, and sustainability. On the Ethisphere.com website, Marc Benioff, chairman and CEO of Salesforce.com, tells the story of an important crossroads reached by the company in 2005.

The young company was already experiencing growing pains from an unexpected number of users and the amount of data they were managing when they discovered that a disk on the server had been installed backward. "It was the kind of mistake," says Benioff, that "happens with an Ikea bookshelf, not a $4 million server. But that doesn't matter. Customers find assigning blame elsewhere off-putting. They didn't want distractions—they wanted gravitas, regret, and humanity."[23]

The initial reaction was to not talk about the problems, but the salesforce team made a radical suggestion: Why not make the system totally open and publish the reliability and transaction rates in real time? It was a novel, possibly dangerous idea, but Benioff decided that "the short-term pain would be worth the long-term gain. Total openness would further drive us to be better."

The website, named "Trust.salesforce.com," went up and the press stories shifted focus away from the service interruptions to the Trust Site itself. Writing for *ZDNet*, Phil Wainewright asked:

Why would Salesforce.com put such sensitive information out there on the Web for all to see? It's all about reputation and trust. Everyone knows that systems do go down from time to time. The only way to restore confidence is to make sure that, if it does happen, customers have the best possible information about what is going on.[24]

"The value of Trust," says Benioff, "was not in the lexicon of business software before. Now, many companies, including Google and Amazon, have adopted their own Trust Sites."[25]

There are other companies, of course, that manage to excel at customer service, but I've used the examples of Zappos and Salesforce.com to illustrate that technology doesn't have to be a barrier to authentic, honest, customer communication. Amazon is the world's largest online retailer, three times as large as its nearest competitor. It's also a consistent winner of a variety of customer service awards and a top-ten winner of *Forbes'* "Most Admired Companies." Many of the things that Amazon does right have little to do with technology. Callers are greeted with a human voice. Amazon.com reminds you that you've already purchased a product and makes sure that you want to buy it again before ringing up another sale. Customers are encouraged to freely evaluate products, or the company, for good or ill. All vendors are subject to a customer satisfaction rating system. Amazon's return and replacement policies are notorious for fairness and fast execution.

These companies are demonstrating that being upfront with customers, which is always the right thing to do, is also a strategy for success. Our customers, like our employees, deserve all the information, both positive and negative, that they need to make well-informed decisions. And they deserve it delivered easily and honestly. It's easy to obfuscate. And the ease of obfuscation may work to one's advantage for a few, maybe quite a few, quick sales. Hidden costs and fees may actually add to bottom line profit. A clouded contract, policy, or offer, written around loopholes or in fine print, may really work to lock customers into lucrative short-term arrangements. But these are Faustian bargains. Misleading customers won't build trust or foster the emotional connections that inspire loyalty for the long haul.

Undercover Bosses

The popular television show, *Undercover Boss*, works for only one reason. The boss is out of touch. As the show often reveals, the Boss has become so far removed from the action that he or she doesn't know the employees, the product or service, or the customers. Now, even in a "reality" show, there's a lot of scripting going on. But the isolated nature of leaders at the top isn't just a fiction created for television drama, especially when it comes to customer service. A recent survey asked the leaders of big companies if they would describe their companies as providing "superior" customer service. The answer, for 80 percent of them, was a definitive "Yes!" When consumers, however, were asked the same question, only 8 percent described these same companies as delivering superior customer service.[26] That's a huge, and revealing, gap in perception. It's one, I submit, that's bound to translate into bad management decisions, poor allocation of company resources, and communications, all the way down the chain, that don't reflect reality. If we don't know that we're not making our customers happy, what in the world *do* we really know?

 The more you engage with customers, the clearer things become and the easier it is to determine what you should be doing.
—John Russell

Whether we're struggling to run a small local business or steering at the helm of a large public one, it's easy to forget, as we go through our days, exactly why we do the work that we do. Often we're focused so hard on *how* we do our jobs that we can almost forget *why*. The why, of course, is the customer. The consumer, the client, the user, or the guest. While direct customer contact may seem very far removed from our day to day responsibilities, we isolate ourselves from it at our peril.

The emotions of our customers are difficult to extract from market research or customer satisfaction surveys, but they can easily be learned from sincere one-on-one dialog. Only when we actually meet and talk with customers in venues that generate honest and open conversation can we learn how customers actually feel about our product or service, and by extension, our company. There's a danger, of course, in getting up front and personal with customers. We risk opening ourselves up to their anger and frustration. We're likely to hear some things that can really hurt. But what we don't know can hurt us more.

Raising the Bar

Sales has never had a good reputation for honesty or sincerity. And technology has now so dehumanized many of our commercial exchanges that the customer service bar is very low. But there's a silver lining in that cloud. It doesn't take so much to stand out these days. We can be different simply by returning to fundamentals. We can create significant competitive advantage by treating our customers as we'd like to be treated.

While top management and C-suite executives are often isolated from the actual customer experience, the most critical team they lead, always, is the customer service team. As we leaders fully absorb this reality, we will begin to see that earning client or customer trust is our single most important job. We'll see all customer communications as Articles of Trust and understand that even the smallest of deceits can sever those bonds of faith. We'll empower all of our employees, from top to bottom, but especially those in the front-line trenches, to communicate transparently and authentically with our customers and to use the intelligence and creativity that we pay them for to solve customer problems. We'll likely find that empowerment engenders trust in them, too, and brings dignity and enthusiasm to their own work.

 There is only one boss. The customer. And he can fire everybody in the company from the chairman on down, simply by spending his money somewhere else.
—Sam Walton

By returning to some of the values of that "once upon a time" era when we did business face-to-face, our word was our bond, and the customer relationship was genuinely valued, we can not only create significant competitive advantage for our own organizations but begin doing our own part to improve the pervasive consumer bad mood. Treating customers well is the job of everyone in the organization, but it's the responsibility of senior management to ingrain the goal of customer trust into the company's culture. The customer service bar is most effectively raised from the top.

DARE!

Even if we don't know where to put them in our pie charts or factor them into our financial models, emotions are as critical to every company's bottom line as they are to a great date, an enduring friendship, or a happy marriage. But leaders can't really know what emotional experiences their customers have until they put on their customer's shoes and walk around in them awhile.

I dare you to go "undercover" with your own company's customers. Call in yourself to your own company's help or call center to see how customers are greeted and treated. Do you dare to take a turn at handling customer complaints yourself? To participate in your own company's social media conversations, under your own name, and with your own title? I dare you to discover for yourself where training or policy is hindering, rather than helping, your customer-facing workforce to build trust and loyalty.

I challenge you also to examine the company's marketing messages, its forms and policies, its sales training scripts, even its product instructions—indeed, every single customer communication that emanates from the company, and to examine these, not from management's point of view, but from the customer's. If there are places where the sincerity is fake, where the words don't align with actions, or where the effort is clearly to obscure and encrypt—to distance the customer from the solution or to maximize short-term profits over long-term customer relationships—then there's a place for decision. But there's also an opportunity point for creating conspicuous distinctions that will set you apart.

I think that customers will pay for those kinds of distinctions. I know that I will.

CHAPTER 7
TRUSTING CORPORATE CULTURES

For more than a century, the traditional model of leadership for American business was autocratic and bureaucratic—a command and control model, characterized by a rigid, hierarchical organizational structure within which standards and procedures were strictly defined. The leader in this system was set above and apart by his position and had unquestionable authority for all decision-making. When orders came down from HQ, the rank and file followed them with the kind of unflinching, unthinking obedience that Alfred, Lord Tennyson described in "The Charge of the Light Brigade":

Theirs not to reason why,
Theirs but to do and die.

It was a highly effective model for manufacturing, well-suited for industrial production where the goal was to achieve a narrow range of objectives in a short period of time and success was measured in material units.

We don't hear the business schools or leadership gurus actively touting the old command and control model much these days. The underlying psychology is unpleasant to us in a more democratized business landscape. We're in a "social" era now, and know that we need "employee engagement" and "people-centered" management styles. We all admit that the old paradigm doesn't suit an information age as well as it did an industrial one.

Changes happen much faster these days. The business and economic environments are far less predictable and we need faster, more flexible ways of problem solving. In the new knowledge economy, the sources of innovative ideas are dispersed throughout many geographical and cultural networks; increasing globalization means that even small businesses are integrated into international networks of suppliers, subcontractors, distributors, and partners. Even without fundamental structural reorganization, we're almost obliged to take a more open, inclusive, and collaborative approach to leadership in order to cope with the challenges and opportunities of a hyper-connected world.

The starting point for this new approach often begins with technology. We buy collaboration software, jump into social media, introduce blogs, wikis, instant messaging, video conferencing, and other network tools to encourage more cooperation, co-working, and idea sharing. In far too many cases, however, these tools and systems don't produce the expected results. Too often, technology is merely an overlay, or an add-on, to some version of the old hierarchical system.

Beneath a veneer of new terms and new technology, the old model still dictates the basis for communication and the paths to connection in many organizations. We still produce our organizational charts, and while their inverted pyramids, circles, bi-directional arrows, and friendlier-sounding titles may conceal the fact, they are still largely hierarchical and meant to reflect that reporting structure. We still operate largely in silos, and too often the notion of teamwork is still to attend the meeting, follow instructions, complete your assigned task, do your job, and stay in your place. In many organizations the concentration of power in still firmly held in the hands of a few people at the top. Leaders are often still isolated from employees and customers. Information is still controlled, and brokered by decree, from the pyramid's narrow apex.

The tools may have changed, but not the fundamentals. The fact that we *can* connect doesn't necessarily make us *feel* connected. No tool can give meaning to our work or provide context for how it fits into the big picture. Nor can tools alone inspire innovation and creativity. And when it comes to genuine employee engagement, there just isn't an app for that.

Communication technologies can certainly enable the type of culture that seems absolutely necessary for a free-flowing digital age—the kind of culture in which information is shared openly and honestly, where all employees feel engaged and valued and inspired to work collaboratively. But the technologies can't create them. Such cultures aren't technology-based. They're principle-based. Without addressing the underlying mindset, it's impossible to create the type of culture that genuinely encourages collaboration and innovation.

If we accept that as top leaders we are the chief influencers of the cultures we lead, then the responsibility for changing that mindset rests squarely on our shoulders. Without the personal conviction that an open communication culture is necessary, not only to business success but also to a more ethical, high-trust workplace, our efforts will likely fail. But senior leaders who are committed to this ideal can signal the change and set the tone. We will need to establish a clear vision of what such a culture will look like and how it will operate. We will have to become proactive connectors of groups, teams, and individuals who have been effectively walled off from one another by bureaucratic management systems. We will need to work seriously to establish an environment of trust that gives voice to everyone in the organization and not only tolerates but encourages the expression of diverse viewpoints and contrary opinions. And, as we start to talk the talk, we'll have to walk the walk, pushing our own egos aside, surrendering much of the spotlight, authority, and power enjoyed by command and control leaders. We'll have to become more open, trusting, and collaborative individuals ourselves.

The Open Communications Vision

Nothing is as vital to the success of every company as the way it manages communications. It's the way we get things done. But too many companies lack a communication vision. We don't orient employees to our communication approach, articulate it as an organizational value, or even include it among our cultural expectations.

Unlike corporate strategy visions, which are frequently narrow, business-oriented statements addressed to the marketplace, a communication vision must be articulated to the workforce. It's the employees, after all, who most need to understand the communication climate and who most need to know the answers to the fundamental questions on which collaboration is based. Questions like

> Is this organization truly committed to transparency, or is that only a hollow corporate values platitude that doesn't align with the reality?

> Can I really expect leaders to provide information in which I have a legitimate interest, or is it brokered from the top?

> Are the discussions between company executives and employees really safe and honest or does the culture actually reward only political correctness and praise for management?

> Is this a culture in which non-confidential and non-proprietary information is actively and freely shared?

Formal communication vision statements can help to answer some of these questions. Here's a great example of a communication vision statement from an Australian non-profit:

> *"Earthwatch Australia is committed to transparency about how we conduct our work to achieve our global mission. This includes being open about our activities, funding sources, expenditure, and partnerships with all stakeholders."*

Here's another from a global web-hosting group:

> *"SoftCom is dedicated to having open, timely, and transparent communications with its community and stakeholders."*

I like these formal, clearly articulated communication vision statements, but there are many ways to drive home the culture's seriousness about open communication. Proactive communication initiatives endorsed by leadership are among the most effective. Some companies manage these extremely well.

At the monthly corporate meetings of international travel company Grand Circle Corp., employees are expected to bring up "non-discussables" and get answers to their questions from the executive team. "Non-discussables" are described by CEO Alan Lewis as "things you don't want to hear," and no topic is off limits. Grand Circle defines "open and courageous communication" as being willing to ask tough questions, give constructive feedback to others, and accept such feedback without defensiveness. It's one of the values that the company lives by.[27]

Cisco Systems is another company that doesn't leave its workforce to guess about the communication vision. Like many other Silicon Valley firms, Cisco has embraced open communication since its origin. The company is quite explicit about its cultural expectations for the workplace. On the back of each employee's ID badge are seventeen cultural components that link the Cisco family to customer success. "Open communication" is listed there, along with other factors like "trust," "empowerment," "innovation," and "fun."

Spreading the Word

There really isn't any medium, forum, venue, or voice that can't be enlisted in articulating the goals and advantages of an open communication culture. From the detailed and explicit description in the company's policies manual to the cartoon over the water cooler that's captioned, "Great ideas are for sharing," the opportunities abound. Leaders need to share the vision of an open communication culture across all locations and business units with every employee. To drive it down throughout the organization we must not only demonstrate it, but speak and write about it often, in multiple ways and in multiple venues and as passionately as we know how.

Although many cultural qualities are necessary to create the proper environment for collaboration, open communication is by far the most important. Unless the goal of open communication is established as a mutual belief and value system, it seems unlikely that any culture can evolve to its Information Age potential. Senior leaders who want to transition away from a command and control model and bring the workforce into active, engaged partnership can be the champions of that transformation, but it takes serious commitment. There's a lot of ground to cover between crafting and publicizing the vision and actually learning to live it.

Open in Name Only?

An open communication policy is not necessarily an honest communication policy. Employees who struggle to reconcile an ostensibly open communication policy with one that is open in name only will be familiar with these situations:

> Non-proprietary communications are still treated as private and you are shamed or punished for passing them on. If you get the scoop from your supervisor, it's privileged. Your own team's progress, or lack of it, is nobody else's business. And don't you dare tweet the meeting!

"Open" meetings, brain-storming sessions, or so-called collaborative initiatives are really invitation only. You should apply and be accepted to attend. The cube walls may have come down, but command and control silos and the Old Boy network are fully operational. Membership is really about as all-inclusive as it is at the local yacht club or *Harvard Law Review*.

You're encouraged to bring up touchy topics and unmentionable subjects. All the corporate propaganda says so. But just try it and feel the room chill. Hear your supervisor clear his throat. Watch the boss fidget with his smartphone. See the agenda move on.

While touting openness and transparency as an organizational value, your boss routinely asks you to lie to your peers, customers, suppliers, or others. The requests usually begin with "Just tell him (her/them) . . ." After that you can fill in the blank:

"Just tell her I'm in a meeting."
"Just tell him that we didn't get his (application/objection/ offer) in time."
"Just tell the customer that this is the last one at that price."
"Just tell the supplier that the discount has expired."
"Just tell them not to report it."

This practice is among the most insidious acids to erode trust. Asking someone to lie for you is unethical. If you're in a position of power, it's bullying. It also serves as an open invitation for others to lie to you.

There's a big difference between "Openness and Honesty" as a slogan in the break room and a truly open communication culture. Nothing confuses people faster than inconsistency. Encouraging employees to be open while systematically conditioning them to do the opposite can only damage trust.

Connectors in Chief

In his bestselling book, *The Tipping Point: How Little Things Can Make a Big Difference*, Malcolm Gladwell introduced the term "connector" to describe people who are especially skilled at playing the intermediary between different social groups. These are people with a special gift for bringing people together, who link us up to one another and to the world.[28] To a great extent, this task of connecting, or forming alliances, has always fallen to the CEO. In the manufacturing economy, those connections were between suppliers, distributors, and partners. In the new knowledge economy, however, the most valuable connections are now between minds. In a global marketplace, and with a workface whose members are increasingly not only culturally diverse but often separated by great physical distance, it's becoming critical that senior leaders become the Connectors in Chief in their organizations. Our challenge today is to harness the collective genius within our organizations.

While working together implies inclusion, inclusion itself takes work. The leader's roll is to break down the walls and silos and to build bridges between previously unconnected people and teams. Yes, of course, this means bringing sales and marketing together, but, as we all know, silos exist beyond departments. They can be cultural, generational, gender based, and geographic. But open—and highly proactive—communication policies, practices, and habits can permeate those walls and silos.

Leadership can enable and inspire the connections that bring people together in new collaborative alliances. Here are a few areas where leaders can function as Connectors in Chief:

Encouraging Introductions

In some large companies, all functional teams are not even aware of one another's existence, let alone of their goals or missions. In that kind of information vacuum, it's difficult to increase efficiencies, eliminate redundancies, and share best practices, lessons learned, or other accumulated knowledge. It's the situation lamented by former Hewlett Packard CEO, Lew Platt: "If only HP knew what HP knows."

This is another area where leadership-endorsed communication initiatives pay off. We can use them to introduce people who share common interests or undiscovered skill sets. We can empower management to create company-wide communities of practice, or to encourage them to form organically. We can bring people together physically when we can, virtually when we can't. These efforts will make employees feel more engaged and foster natural collaboration.

Connecting to the Community

Community service projects offer exceptional opportunities for bringing people together to bond with one another and with the wider world. Andy Garber, who is now managing director of Strategy and Operation for Deloitte Consulting LLP, knows just how important these efforts can become to the workforce and the community, even when they start quite small.

Back in 1998, Andy was in charge of Deloitte's Atlanta office when a small group of third-year employees came to him with an idea. They wanted to do a community service project. They'd found an overrun park they wanted to clean up. They wanted to build benches and install swing sets, put in new plants, and make paths through the park.

Deloitte was small in Atlanta back then, and in Andy's words, "This was a huge risk for a lot of reasons. It cost around $50,000 just to fund the project and then, of course, we were taking everybody out for a day and there were all the lost opportunities that accompanied that. To do something for the community, we were going to have to turn our own world upside down."

But Andy said yes, and eight hundred people showed up for that one day. The effort grew into an annual community service project in which over 100,000 Deloitte employees now participate. As Andy has learned, there's almost no limit to how large a community service project can become.

Jo Pamphile, president of the T. Howard Foundation, also knows how important an organization's willingness to share time and resources with the community can be. Sometimes it can even save lives. Here's the story Jo told me about her own experience:

In 2005, I was working in a for-profit organization when Hurricane Katrina struck New Orleans. My project was based in Baton Rouge, but because we were a customer service operation, I got the call requesting help in setting up an emergency hotline for victims to communicate and to connect to emergency services.

I first got in touch with Business Development to see if I had budget constraints. The answer was no. This was an easy sell because this had always been a mission-driven organization. Next, I contacted Tech Support, who was able to quickly set us up with a toll free number. The Call Center agreed to handle volunteers. By 4:00 that afternoon we had gone live. At the height of the need we were handling twenty thousand calls a day. There's no doubt that what we were able to do saved lives. We were able to help not just because we had the resources, but because leadership had always felt a connection and responsibility to the greater community.

Monitoring Diversity Messaging

Trusting corporate cultures view diversity as an opportunity for enrichment, not as a problem to be solved. There's a big difference between a workforce that hears, "We've got to work together," and one that hears, "We get to work together." When top management communicates pride in the company's diversity and enthusiasm for creating new mixes, bringing in outsiders, and hearing ideas from everyone, much of the fear of collaboration will disappear and trust will replace it.

Embracing the Tools

The new networking technologies do enable us to bridge the barriers of both distance and hierarchy, but everyone needs to buy into the tools so that they, and the teams they can benefit, work together. That means everyone. Senior executives are not always the most tech-savvy people in the organization. (I speak from experience here.) But we need to use the tools ourselves. Even if that means Facebook and Twitter. Social media can also provide a valuable feedback mechanism for allowing employees to inter-act directly with the CEO.

We can't expect the workforce to adopt behaviors that we're avoiding. We may have to learn to communicate more spon-taneously. And at first, we're likely to feel exposed by all that transparency and sharing. But if we want to encourage the rapid sharing of ideas and discover new ways of working, we must participate ourselves.

Making Face Time

Finally, it's a great advantage to organizations when their leaders work to make themselves visible and to connect personally with teams and individuals who are not normally in their immedi-ate reporting sphere. I'm a big fan of Management By Walking Around (MBWA) and find that making "face time" to get to know others helps to build relationships beyond the constraints of my official role. Leaders need to get out of the ivory tower now and then and be visible to those they lead. We shouldn't be afraid to share ourselves with your employees and dialog with them honestly about problems and opportunities. Getting out of our own personal silos can provide the leadership that encourages others to do the same.

Setting the Example

The best way for leaders to see that information flows freely in their organizations is to set a good example. That means no bro-kering, but it also means consistently demonstrating that we have the courage to seek out and accept unsettling information. The cultural norm will begin to shift toward transparency when we demonstrate the behaviors we want our employees to mirror.

Safety Engineering

At its core, an open and collaborative environment requires far higher levels of trust than a command and control environment because we must surrender some level of control and increase our dependence on the people we are collaborating with. I've stressed the importance of leaders themselves becoming worthy of trust, but as we've already noted, trust is self-perpetuating. In order for trust to become ingrained as a core dynamic in the corporate culture, leaders must be able to extend it, too. John Mackey, CEO of Whole Foods, makes this important point in writing on the subject of "Creating the High Trust Organization":

> Many leaders make the mistake of believing that the key to increasing organizational trust is to somehow get the workforce to trust the leadership more. While this is obviously very important, it is equally important that the leadership trust the workforce. To receive trust, it is usually necessary that we give trust. Organizing into small interlocking teams helps ensure that trust will flow in all directions within the organization— upwards, downwards, within the team, and across teams.[29]

Trust is very much a two-way street. We can't empower our teams to unleash their creative potential or find real enthusiasm for their work unless we trust them to do it. When we operate on the assumption that members of the workforce genuinely *want* the business to succeed and will willingly assume responsibility and accountability for what we're trusting them to do, we bring them into true partnership.

Expecting the Best

People rise or fall to our expectations. When we expect positive results we're much more likely to get them. Indra Nooyi, chairman and CEO of Pepsi, calls this presumptive attitude "positive intent." She described how it works in an interview with *Fortune* magazine:

> Whatever anybody says or does, assume positive intent. You will be amazed at how your whole approach to a person or problem becomes very different. When you assume negative intent, you're angry. If you take away that anger and assume positive intent, you will be amazed. Your emotional quotient goes up because you are no longer almost random in your response. You don't get defensive. You don't scream. You are trying to understand and listen because at your basic core you are saying, "Maybe they are saying something to me that I'm not hearing." So "assume positive intent" has been a huge piece of advice for me.[30]

I find Nooyi's advice and the concept of "positive intent" particularly valuable in dealing with a cross-generational and multicultural workforce. Reserving judgment on generational or cultural differences in language, customs, or communication and work styles keeps us open to learning. It's an extension of trust in its own right.

Modeling Authentic Conversations

My friends and coworkers hear me lament it all the time: "*Nobody talks to anybody anymore!*" And it's true that I'm more than a little worried. Particularly about the young, who increasingly communicate in short blurbs on social media, or by IM or cell phone, through truncated fragments of alphabet, devoid of grammar, syntax, or what we once called "spelling." "*Conversation is a dying art!*" I complain. And for some, perhaps, it really is dead. But I wouldn't agitate so much if I were really resigned. Implicit in my complaint is that word, "art," and the conviction that, like other arts, the art of conversation is worth practicing and preserving.

 To have real conversation with people may seem like such a simple, obvious suggestion, but it involves courage and risk.
—Thomas Moore

Most of us still want to talk to one another. And most of us know that spontaneous, natural conversation is the best way to relate to our friends, spouses, and others in our personal lives. In conversation in our personal relationships, we simply want to know the other person—to share, learn, explore, and build trust. We still have to do a lot of talking in business, too, but here the situation is different. Especially for leaders. In our business conversations we're agenda-driven, time-constrained, and goal-oriented. In other words, we want something. We're certain that we can only get what we want when we control the process.

Our audiences, of course, know this and immediately set up barriers and defenses. They know they're going to be lectured to, asked to comply, required to be silent, or to respond according to protocol or the Q&A bullet points that the agenda dictates. They fully expect to become "objects" of our communication, not participants in anything approaching a dynamic dialog. For very good reason, they may think they already know what we're going to say, and can play BS bingo while we rattle on.

Maybe we can't change everything. We can't have one-on-one, sit-down conversations with everyone with whom we need to communicate. We still have to attend meetings and presentations and send company-wide memos. But just as there are ways to make our face-to-face conversations more authentic, there are methods for making other corporate communications more closely resemble the more flexible, authentic nature of genuine dialog. Conversation is an art, so we can get better at it. And we can use many of its best techniques to restore the trust-building process to other communications.

Learning to Listen

We all like to think of ourselves as good listeners, but few of us actually are. The truth is that most of us only listen about 25 percent of the time. Typically we have only listened to the first three or four words of a sentence before we have begun formulating our own response. We listen, in other words, for the next opportunity to talk.

 Listening is a magnetic and strange thing, a creative force. The friends who listen to us are the ones we move toward, and we want to sit in their radius. When we are listened to, it creates us, makes us unfold and expand.
—Karl Menninger

Active listening is not just a buzz phrase. It's a communication technique that works and pays enormous dividends to those who employ it. Active listening has been the subject of many books and a component of many leadership development courses and workshops. It's a prime area of self-development for leaders to undertake with a trained coach or counselor. Here's a brief summary of active listening skills:

1. ***Attend fully***: Maintain eye contact. Don't fail to listen because you're thinking about what you're going to say next. Assume positive intent. Avoid prejudging. Keep an open mind.
2. ***Restate and paraphrase***: Ask questions for clarification; restate or paraphrase the speaker's point to make sure that you didn't misunderstand.
3. ***Interpret and confirm***: Respond to the message by offering a tentative interpretation of the speaker's feelings, desires, or meanings.
4. ***Allow for space and silence***: Don't panic in the pauses or be tempted to fill them with glib, easy sound bites. Listening demands space in a communication exchange. It requires giving each of you time to think as well as to talk. And confident, self-reflective leaders aren't afraid of saying, "You know, I'm not sure about what you are suggesting. Let me process this for a day or two and get back to you."

Distilled to its essence, active listening requires us to use our eyes, our ears, and our hearts in the service of true communication. While these skills are absolutely vital to one-on-one conversations, active listening also applies to meetings and conversations within groups and teams. As our listening skills improve, so will our aptitude for authentic conversation. Our exchanges, even in meetings and with teams, will become more efficient, more meaningful, less contentious, and more collaborative.

Being Yourself

The suggestion that conversations can be improved by "being yourself" may sound overly simplistic, particularly in light of all the advice out there about discovering your communication "style." At Speakeasy, we work on style, too, inasmuch as that work helps leaders to evaluate, define, and then improve their own unique ability to more powerfully deliver their own personal messages. But we're also fond of telling our clients that the single most important thing you can do to improve the impact of your communication is to stop trying to find the single most important thing! It's the full continuum that counts. But it begins when you speak from your inner voice—who you really are. And who you really are isn't scripted. It isn't locked into a presentation.

David Cummings is the CEO and cofounder of Pardot Marketing Automation. He's now an experienced speaker and presenter. But he wasn't always. Fortunately, David learned early on that the best thing to bring to a presentation is yourself. Here's David's story of one of the most important and successful speeches of his life:

> There I was, a twenty-something CEO of a small software company presuming to present my startup to a group of six hundred investors. I knew I'd be at a disadvantage on that

stage. I was self-funded, with no proven track record, and fifteen years younger than the average presenter. I felt very vulnerable, but I didn't know how to be anybody but myself.

Six minutes doesn't seem long until 1,200 eyeballs are all focused on you. I took a deep breath, focused on speaking slowly and clearly, and tried to connect with the audience. Apparently it worked. When the yellow light in front of me went on indicating that I had thirty seconds left, I looked around, smiled, and said thank you. They were smiling back.[31]

Simple and Sincere

If there's anything at all that corporate America should have observed from the dynamic, zany, creative, and quirky phenomena that is the World Wide Web, it's how people like to talk to one another. It's not in the dull, stale monologue of most corporate communications. While we keep hearing, over and over again, that the web, and especially social media, has created a global "conversation," we're not taking the hint. We now employ the technologies that give our communications a sophisticated look and allow us to disseminate them broadly, but the voice that speaks from them is still too often the boring, authoritarian voice of command and control, devoid of human tone and personal touch.

Individual leaders, and their companies, need to worry less about looking and sounding professional and more about being personal. Simple messaging and personal appeal is what draws others to us in conversation and engenders their trust. Keeping it simple doesn't mean patronizing or talking down to your audience. It means speaking authentically from your own true voice. Leaders who model sincerity and simplicity will find that sincerity and simplicity increase exponentially within the organization. When we allow for verve and wit, a little humor, even irreverence, in the workplace, we're also likely to find that everyone is having more fun.

Choosing the Channel

We have lots of channels for communicating now, but my sense is that we're often a little hasty, or a little lazy, in matching the channel to the demands of the message. Obviously we want to use the technology at our disposal, but choices are important and they have to be made appropriately. We don't want to just automatically pick the handiest or our favorite medium, or fall back on the "I don't have time" excuse to avoid the personal conversation or the private phone call. These are compromises that can damage trust.

With teleconferencing, Skype, Telepresence, and global conference calls, technology has wrought a sea change in the way people hold meetings. These capabilities save companies millions in annual travel costs and allow us to have a fairer approximation of the face-to-face conversation than written communication can offer. But coming across effectively in a virtual gathering is tricky. Most C-suite executives today "grew up" with in-person meetings where everyone was seated around a table in the same room, so a virtual meeting can be a strange environment in which many are still not comfortable. A recent poll taken by Speakeasy found that while 67 percent of senior managers expect to have more virtual meetings in the future, almost 62 percent of them are concerned about their own skill at making the most of these meetings.

The risks in blowing it are real. Too many virtual meetings are data dumps, where one person—usually the highest-ranking person—dominates the discussion. It's frustrating for everyone else, and it's dangerous for leaders because if you give people no opportunity to comment, you really have no idea whether you're missing vital feedback or even if real communication has actually taken place. In that respect, at least, virtual meetings are not that different from the in-person kind. One way to make sure that everyone has a chance to speak up is to appoint a host or moderator who will chime in and ask attendees for their views. This also has the salutary side effect of discouraging too much multitasking. No one wants to be caught not paying attention when called on for a comment. At the very least, the conferencing software should allow for attendees to signal their questions or input. These mechanisms can bring our virtual conversations significantly closer to dialog.

Rewards and Recognition

We can't expect people to flourish in open environments or to eagerly collaborate across teams and business units if criteria for rewards and recognition are only based on individual performance. Changing incentives to include demonstrated collaborative contributions is a big shift away from command and control. There's no magic formula or one-size-fits-all solution for doing it. Each company or organization must find its own methods. I can't speak to the material rewards of raises, bonuses, and promotions, but I can speak to the immaterial ones, which are actually much more important. For decades, poll after poll after poll has revealed the discrepancy between what management *thinks* employees want most and what they *do* actually want. Newsflash: *It's not money!*

While management consistently rates higher wages as the number one workforce motivator, it's actually number five, behind

1. Full appreciation for work done,
2. Feeling part of things,
3. Sympathetic help on personal issues, and
4. Job security.

To my way of thinking, this discrepancy reveals an extremely sad and wholly unnecessary management failure. It leads me to wonder if most leaders don't just find it easier to authorize a bonus than to deliver a pat on the back.

If we really want an engaged workforce, and if we decide, at last, to believe what our employees are telling us, then leaders must assume the responsibility for meeting the simple, human desire for recognition and appreciation. That responsibility is even more pronounced in collaborative environments where team achievement may be taken for granted and where individual achievement is often subsumed by the team's. Leaders have many options for showing appreciation, from creating traditional awards and ceremonies to allowing for zany or specialized *esprit de corps* celebrations to extending personal congratulations and handwritten thank-you notes. The most important is the communications task of broadcasting the success to the organization at large and in the context of larger organizational goals. Everyone should get to feel "a part of things" and everyone should know how each small piece fits into the greater puzzle.

Those feelings of being valued and appreciated come easier to a workforce whose leaders have caught the collaborative spirit themselves—those who most naturally share power and influence and the spotlight of recognition. This can be hard for executives and senior managers whose leadership styles were forged in command and control environments. For charismatic or celebrity leaders, it may be all but impossible. But highly self-aware leaders see their real mission as one of making leaders of others. They don't miss opportunities to credit and reinforce leadership potential.

Coleman Breland, the COO of Turner Network Sales, recently shared with me a particularly vivid example of true collaborative leadership. His story illustrates how powerfully a mature, unselfish leader can engender trust and nurture others just by sharing the spotlight.

It was about two years ago. Our five-person team was involved in tremendously intense and stressful content distribution negotiations with a major cable TV distributor. We'd already been camped out for seven days and were coming to the end of the negotiations. There were only four points left on the table and the Senior VP had the solutions. He could easily have presented his answers and emerged as the hero of the whole long, grueling ordeal. Instead, at my suggestion, he did something incredibly selfless. He turned to another, more junior team member, and said, "Why don't you take these last two points and close out the deal?"

It was 5:30 in the morning and all of us were exhausted, but suddenly everyone was completely energized and exited. The aura in that room became positively electric. We were all deeply moved by the idea that he wanted to share credit and that he would turn over the thrill and the rush, as well as the learning opportunity, of closing out the deal to someone else.

Our already good team became a great team that day. Everyone who was in that room will trust that leader forever.[32]

For me, Coleman's story illustrates an important difference
between good leaders and great ones. It's one thing to be gra-
cious to those who stand in the shadow of our leadership. It's
something else entirely to move aside so that the light can shine
on others.

DARE!

A collaborative, Information-Age organization requires higher
levels of trust than command and control structures demanded.
While our workforce comes to us with well-honed technology
skills, they also bring expectations of openness, fairness, and recognition. But a trusting corporate culture doesn't just happen.
It's built from the top down.

Visioning

In trusting corporate cultures the workforce knows how information is managed. I dare you to examine your commitment
to an open communication culture to determine how far you're
willing to go in articulating it, disseminating it, and consistently
living its vision.

Connecting

To harness the creative power within our organizations, top leaders must become Connectors in Chief. I dare you to assume the
responsibility for becoming a proactive connector, fostering conversations across the entire organization and linking people and

teams across generations and cultures. I challenge you also to consider your organization's connections to the community as part of that charge. I dare you to make yourself more visible to those you lead.

Safety Engineering

Those who want to lead an open and collaborative corporate culture are obliged to become their organization's safety engineers. I dare you to make extending trust and establishing safety an organizational priority. I dare you to value the art of conversation and to make active listening a skill you want to develop and model. I dare you to risk your unmasked self in corporate conversations and model simplicity and sincerity for others.

Rewards and Recognition

The workforce's need for recognition and belonging are not different from our own. I dare you to be that rare leader who generously praises and joyfully celebrates workforce achievements. Do you dare to share the spotlight, power, and influence of your own leadership in the interest of developing others?

CHAPTER 8
IS BUSINESS EVIL?

I began this volume by expressing my concerns about the global trust fall and its ominous implications for our society and the future. Obviously, many forces and institutions are culpable in this free fall of trust, not the least of which is our own government. There is little doubt, however, that the general public assigns the lion's share of blame to business and to a vision of success that seems unconstrained by the widespread misery that success might bring down on others. It's all too easy to see how expressions like "crony capitalism," "predatory lending," and "vulture capitalists" have gained currency, and why many believe that business, especially big business, has become profoundly immoral. As we survey the roles of the unemployed, the foreclosed homes and underwater mortgages, or recall the massive environmental damage wrought in the Mississippi gulf, it's not so easy to be optimistic about how we'll reverse the decline in trust.

Indeed, average Americans are not just losing faith in financial institutions, but in the entire free market system. When global polling company GlobeScan first initiated tracking in 2002, four in five Americans (80 percent) saw the free market as the best economic system for the future—the highest level of support among twenty-five countries tracked. Support started to fall away in the following years and has plummeted since 2009, falling fifteen points in a year so that fewer than three in five (59 percent) now see free market capitalism as the best system for the future. This drop makes public support for the free market economy in America lower than in China.

"America," said GlobeScan Chairman Doug Miller, "is the last place we would have expected to see such a sharp drop in trust in the free enterprise system. This is not good news for business."[33]

We've seen systemic criticism in the Occupy Wall Street movement, too, which, in spite of its lack of political coherence, has struck a raw nerve in focusing attention on income equality and substantially altered the national political debate. And in ways we've not seen since perhaps the 1930s, many of our brightest scholars, journalists, and economists are also challenging our most hallowed assumptions about capitalism.

In the title of his article for *The New York Times*, Thomas B. Edsall, professor of journalism at Columbia University, asks, "Is this the End of Free Market Democracy?" Specifically, Edsall wonders if it's "possible that in the United States and Europe, democratic free market capitalism is no longer capable of providing broadly shared benefits to a solid majority of workers?" Edsall cites other highly respected experts who are raising similar questions. Among them are Jeffrey Sachs, a professor at Columbia University; Nobel Prize winner Michael Spence; Francis Fukuyama, senior fellow at Stanford University's Center on Democracy; former Treasury Secretary Lawrence

Summers; and three of the nation's foremost labor economists, Richard Freeman and Lawrence Katz, both of Harvard University, and David Autor of MIT.[34]

Robert Jensen is a professor in the School of Journalism and director of the Senior Fellows Honors Program of the College of Communication at the University of Texas at Austin. Jensen is unambiguous in his criticism of capitalism, condemning it as "inhuman, anti-democratic, and unsustainable."[35]

These are not commie, pinko, hippie radicalists. They are serious thinkers raising serious questions. Some are even business leaders themselves. In a recent *Wall Street Journal* article, Paul Polman, CEO of Unilever, admitted that, "Our version of capitalism has reached its sell-by date." I agree with Polman, gloomy as that may sound. But I agree also with the rest of Polman's comment: "Never has the opportunity for business to shape a more equitable future been so great."[36]

I still have faith in a market economy. Obviously, I don't think business is evil, and I don't think the recent recession, bad as it was, proves the failure of capitalism. I do believe, however, that our system must change and adapt, not only to address many of the issues raised by these thinkers, but to restore the trust that will ensure its survival. I'm still convinced that a "free" market is the best means of providing broad benefits to society at large, but, as we're fond of telling our children, with freedom comes responsibility.

Must Business Do Good?

In *The Wealth of Nations*, Adam Smith made a clear case for the profit motive when he wrote that, "It is not from the benevolence of the butcher, the brewer, or the baker that we expect our dinner, but from their regard to their own self-interest." Smith argued that the pursuit of profits was self-justifying, but that markets were led, as if by an invisible hand, to do what is best for the world.

There are not too many of us left standing who still hold unquestioning faith in the "invisible hand" of the market to reliably do what is best for society's economic interests, let alone to protect our health, safety, or the planet's limited resources. Even Smith, and later apostles like Milton Friedman (who called social responsibility "a basically subversive doctrine"), sneaked in a few qualifiers. Smith allowed that the invisible hand worked best as long as it supported domestic industry over foreign, and Friedman qualified his thesis that "the social responsibility of business is to increase profits" with "*as long as you play by the rules.*"[37]

Given unanticipated phenomena like off-shoring and the multinational corporation, Smith would readily acknowledge that the whole domestic/foreign thing has become pretty tricky. And of Freidman, whose death preceded the financial meltdown, we have to ask, "*Whose rules?*" When the normal risks of doing business can be erased by government fiat and taxpayer dollars, rules have no meaning. When it's all too easy to dance on the knife edge of what is legally permissible, the rules have become too complex and obscure. In the recent wake of surprise losses by one of its trading groups, JPMorgan Chase CEO Jamie Dimon said, "I have no idea whether we broke the law."[38] When the rules can be ignored with impunity, they have no force. The absence, so far, of any criminal convictions for identified financial or environmental crimes is a source of rage for many and evidence that the rules don't apply fairly to all.

Even though we may begin to offset some of the deregulation of the '80s and '90s, I don't think the public will be placated by a new spate of rules superimposed on business. What the public wants to see is change from the inside out.

> ⓘ **Ends and means are inseparable. You cannot make a worthy end with an unworthy means.**
> **—Stephen R. Covey**

The question of "Must business do good in the world?" is becoming moot. The answer is *yes!* Because it has to. It has to if our economy, our democracy, and even the smaller and smaller planet on which we *all* do business, is going to survive.

Whether we're comfortable with the idea or not, every business is a community, one that is part of larger local and national communities and ultimately the global one. While we may not be shareholders, we are all stakeholders in the social, economic, and environmental ecosystems that we share. It no longer makes sense for business to persist in exploiting and alienating its communities. In the short term, we're shooting ourselves in the foot. In the long term, if the problems that pervade these shared ecosystems aren't solved, "business" has no more future than the rest of us.

The idea that businesses must choose between making a profit and being good local, national, and global citizens has always presented a fallacy of false choice anyway—one that more and more leaders are recognizing. Richard Branson of the UK's Virgin companies is one of the most respected business leaders in the world. He is also the author of the provocatively titled *Screw Business as Usual*, in which he describes a long list of multinational companies that are managing to do both. A few of them are Salesforce.com, which gives away one percent of its time, product, and equity to charity, Shell's GroFin initiative which incubates small businesses in Africa, and General Electric's ecomagination commitment to developing clean-tech products. (GE's original $5 billion investment has generated $70 billion in revenue.)

But Branson also describes many small, entrepreneurial startups, many in third world countries, which are providing products and services that do well in the marketplace and also do good for the world. "A good, socially aware business doesn't have to be big to make an impact," says Branson, "it just has to have the right people in place." [39] Branson is throwing his energies, wealth, and vast business knowledge into this new kind of enlightened capitalism—Capitalism 24902, he calls it, for the circumference of the planet, measured in miles.

John Mackey, the Whole Foods CEO whose wisdom I've already shared, is another of those leaders who doesn't see doing good and doing well as an "either/or" proposition. Here Mackey addresses the fallacy of assuming that animal ethics and financial success are at opposing poles:

> I think one of the most misunderstood things about business in America is that people are either doing things for altruistic reasons or they are greedy and selfish, just after profit. That type of dichotomy portrays a false image of business. It certainly is a false image of Whole Foods. The whole idea is to do both: the animals have to flourish, but in such a way that it'll be cheap enough for the customers to buy it. [40]

Business and societal interests are not mutually exclusive. The public doesn't think so. Our customers don't think so. Our employees, more and more of whom are reluctant to spend their working lives solely to enrich owners or anonymous stockholders, don't think so, either. Younger workers especially want to participate in serving some greater good. If they perceive our organization as only creating problems, never solutions, they'll go elsewhere.

Doing Well While Doing Good

There's reason to hope that one day we can scrap this false dilemma of capitalism. New forms of purpose-driven businesses are emerging to combine profit-making with responses to social and environmental issues, and highly traditional businesses are also discovering that they can create economic value in ways that correspond to creating value for society.

Cause marketing, which is the collaboration between a corporation and a nonprofit, is increasingly being employed by companies to build reputation and brand loyalty and to attract target customers, while simultaneously benefitting the non-profit's cause. American Express first used the phrase and demonstrated the mutual benefits of cause marketing in 1983 with its campaign to raise money for the Statue of Liberty's restoration. American Express donated one penny to the restoration every time someone used its charge card. As a result, the number of new cardholders grew by 45 percent, and card usage increased by 28 percent. Hundreds, perhaps thousands, of companies today are using the same model to connect with customers while simultaneously doing good. Efforts like these can backfire if our customers or the public discovers that we've been deceptive or insincere, but any business with its head, and heart, in the right place can employ this approach in its community.

Even the strict legal dichotomy between "for-profit" organizations created simply to make money and "non-profit" entities whose mission is to do good is beginning to blur. Earlier this year the state of California joined Vermont, Maryland, New York, New Jersey, Virginia, and Hawaii in legally allowing companies to specify they are pursuing social good as well as shareholder value in their charters. Benefit corporation (B Company) bills have also been introduced in Colorado, North Carolina, Pennsylvania, and Michigan. We may soon see an explosion of these new types of corporations that harness the power of business to solve social and environmental problems. To my way of thinking, this is an all-around win for business and for community.

Businesses in the abstract, like humans in the particular, are complicated, self-interested, and fallible. But there is nothing that says either is intrinsically destructive, deceitful, or inherently irresponsible. Neither operates in a moral vacuum, cut off from social context and immune to the human repercussions of our actions. There is no foundational incompatibility between doing business ethically and transparently and getting good financial results. We don't have to choose. We can do both.

Being Good to Do Well

I'm convinced that every business can serve the greater good. We don't need to have rich philanthropic arms or vast political influence to do it. Every company, even the smallest, can find some way to serve, and to balance some taking with some giving. It could be as simple as sponsoring a small charity or giving employees time off for community service, or even just fixing up a local park. But my larger focus has been on even more fundamental actions that we can take to become better corporate citizens, more effective leaders, and happier, more congruent individuals. We can rebuild trust by returning to time-honored ethical norms and leading from within a moral framework—by being "good" in ways that any five-year-old could understand.

Institutional accountability and financial transparency is an obvious starting point, and there's plenty of evidence accumulating to suggest that being upfront with investors and analysts makes good business sense. No less an expert than Samuel DiPiazza, CEO of PricewaterhouseCoopers, thinks that honesty and transparency actually pay off. In *Building Public Trust: The Future of Corporate Reporting,* DiPiazza shows that fuller disclosure wins more trust from investors, reducing risk and translating into higher valuations.[41] Research in foreign markets, too, shows a statistically significant decline in borrowing costs when reporters choose to become more transparent.[42]

For five years now, *Forbes* magazine has worked with GMI Ratings to analyze more than eight thousand companies that trade on U.S. exchanges. GMI has reported that its One Hundred Most Trustworthy Companies have consistently demonstrated transparent and conservative accounting practices.[43]

I'm inclined to believe the trend of these findings. We've all had enough of fabricated truth, half-truth, and blatant financial falsehoods. The company might grow faster than you think when its financial reporting becomes transparent, relevant, and reliable. Employees, too, deserve financial transparency. The natural inclination to keep the institution's finances, even its financial problems, confined to the C-suite is self-defeating if we want our workforce to feel a real sense of ownership.

Financial transparency, however, is just part of the change that the public, our customers, and our employees need to see. I have also argued for greater transparency in marketing and internal business communications and conversations, using the term as a human value or virtue to express the necessary truthfulness to which those who trust us are entitled. To the extent that employees understand how and why things are done, the more their trust increases. To the extent that we preach, and practice, open communication cultures, fear, paralysis, and resentment dissipate in the workplace. We enjoy better employee retention and create the motivation for innovation and collaboration.

Our customers, too, deserve to see a lot more transparency and truth-telling. I have tried to make the case for less camouflage, doublespeak, and deception in marketing and customer communications, and also for our buying public's deep desire to do business with companies who are working to create value beyond pure profit. But the jury on this issue is already coming in. With the growth of the internet and the focusing influences of social media, two billion pairs of eyes are now watching us. They're paying serious attention to what we say and do, and will find the gaps between the hype and the facts. No public relations campaign can do enough spinning, whitewashing, or greenwashing to long overcome that kind of scrutiny. We have no choice but to become more open, honest, and trustworthy to create and retain loyal customers.

For leaders themselves there is everything to be gained in resisting the old power stereotypes and discarding the masks that prevent us from genuinely connecting to others. There is less personal conflict, less discrepancy between the personal/business self and the work/home self. Freeing up all that energy releases the passion that enables us not just to succeed, but to thrive in our professions, and to infect the entire organization with that passion. There is always a price to pay for sublimating the self, but leaders exact a toll on others, too, when the expression of honest emotion and human vulnerability is sacrificed in the interest of protecting a false persona. I raise this issue here at the end, as I did in the beginning, because it frames and informs everything I know, or think I know, about the dynamics of leadership. It precipitated my own personal self-examination, led to my own career in business communications, and it still directs everything we do at Speakeasy in our attempt to help businesses articulate their messages and strengthen their messengers.

Becoming as Good as Our Word

There is little question that significant change may be required to restore confidence in the financial sector especially, in business generally, and, for many, in the very economic system that thus far has sustained our democracy. Some say we need nothing less than a revolution. That may be. But I would like to think that the most constructive revolution might come from within the business sector itself.

The financial crisis has created a window of opportunity for business leaders to imagine how our organizations might do things differently. Were we to embrace the conviction that a better business world is a better world for all, we might bring about a genuine ethical revolution—one that recovers the moral ground that has been so damagingly lost these last years. It will undoubtedly take time. A great deal of damage has been done. But the magnitude and complexity of the task before us is the worst reason for postponing action.

Should the global public begin to see American businesses taking concrete steps to reduce fraud and improve institutional accountability and transparency, the needle of cynicism will move. When our PR departments and professional communicators start to shift the emphasis from "managing" public perceptions to communicating our sincerely held values, our clear higher purpose, and even our valiant struggles and honest failures, we'll start to refill the reservoir of trust. Even when the challenges are tough budget issues or overcoming crises, we'll fare better in being frank with the people than by trying to spin our way out of trouble.

When our customers begin finding more alignment between what we say and what we do, their mood will improve. We'll be spending less energy and fewer resources on defense, and more on really helping our customers to make the best use of our products and services. Through a more genuine dialog, we'll make those products and services better, and glean new, innovative ideas for the future.

When our employees sense that the old "We vs. Them" battleground has been replaced by a more collaborative playing field where communications are open, safe, and honest, we're bound to have a more engaged and energized workforce.

When business schools start to discuss character as well as strategy, and begin to emphasize ethics as the *absolute* foundation for good business, we'll have turned an important corner. Tomorrow's leaders would begin their apprenticeships with a concept of value that doesn't come at the expense of people, our planet, or their own integrity.

Pie in the sky? Maybe. But these are the changes that the public, our customers, and our employees are asking for, and change from within seems a better remedy than forced change through government. Should business step up to lead such a revolution, I don't think our political leaders could fail to take notice. Most important, I don't think our youth could fail to notice. Perhaps business could succeed where government, the media, academia, and even our religious leaders have failed to provide our young with new mental models of trustworthiness and integrity.

In the final analysis, ethics is about individual people making individual choices. Ethical policies don't even make it into the employee handbook, let alone get translated in active, ongoing, felt, and experienced practice, unless one, or many, individuals have made conscious choices. Behavior in an organization is a cumulative accretion over time. That behavior works to build trust or to destroy it. The conscious decisions made by the leaders at the top—decisions that are witnessed and generalized across the organization—make all the difference.

One Voice at a Time

Each of us sees the world through the prism of our own interests and concerns. My own is communication, and admittedly I've devoted much attention to implicating deceptive, unethical, and inauthentic communication practices in the global trust fall. Given that I've assigned so much blame to communication deficits and deceptions, readers may be wondering why the CEO of a professional communications company has not offered more in the way of techniques, tips, or skill-building exercises—specific "how to" steps for achieving excellence in communication. That, perhaps, is the subject of another book. This one was written in the hope of inspiring what no one can really teach.

At Speakeasy, we know absolutely that communication excellence is a combination of birthright, art, and craft. Some people are undeniably, even genetically, better at it than others. Some are more attractive than others, making the ability to look at and to listen to them a little bit easier, and sometimes downright enchanting. Some speakers have stentorian voices, an inherited tone and range that enables them to project to the far corners of a room. Some communicators have rhetorical skills and writing talent, the better able to craft a more persuasive document or speech. Some have the earned advantage of good education, travel, or experiences that inform their words and make their delivery more authoritative.

All of these variables influence communications effectiveness and each can be strengthened and developed for more improvement. Would I say that anybody can be turned into a world-class communicator? That might be far-reaching. But everybody can learn to be a better one. Each of us has the opportunity when we walk into a room to make a difference. And each of us can capitalize on, and magnify, the single greatest strength we have: Everyone has the ability to use their voice to tell the truth. Every one of us has the ability to make our word good. And to choose to be as good as that word.

Do we dare?

ABOUT THE AUTHOR

Scott Weiss centers his life around delivering and driving authentic communication.

From its three offices in Atlanta, New York, and San Francisco, his company, Speakeasy (www.SpeakeasyInc.com), works each year with some 4,500 executives and 350 client companies across five continents.

In addition to speaking engagements with audiences as unique as an international delegation of educators at the Carter Center in Atlanta, many organizations frequently turn to Scott for perspective on issues around trust in leadership. He has been featured in *Forbes, Fortune, Inc.,* CNN Money, and *Investor's Business Daily.*

Weiss started his career on Wall Street and later moved to Turner Broadcasting System (Time Warner), where he spent ten years as an executive vice president in charge of domestic satellite distribution for CNN, TNT and all Turner networks. He founded and directed Turner Private Networks, where he pioneered the creation and launch of the CNN Airport Channel in forty airports worldwide.

Scott serves on the Metro Atlanta Chamber of Commerce, Emory University's board of visitors, and on the board of the Atlanta chapter of Entrepreneurs' Organization. He is the founder and chairman emeritus of the T. Howard Foundation, a Washington, DC–based nonprofit that for the past twenty years has been driving diversity in the media industry through its highly respected mentoring and intern program. He has been a member of the Academy of Television Arts and Sciences and voted in the Emmys for more than two decades.

Weiss lives with his wife of twenty-seven years, Marci, outside Atlanta, Georgia, and is the father of three adult children.

You can catch up with Scott anytime on Twitter (@ScottSpeakeasy) and find out more about his company, Speakeasy, at **www.SpeakeasyInc.com**.

ABOUT SPEAKEASY

For over forty years, Speakeasy has provided personal growth, communication development, and consulting services to some of the most influential business leaders in the world.

There is a unifying philosophy that underpins everything the company does. It's a belief that our focus must always remain on the individual—that everything that individual needs to be a great communicator already exists within them. Our work is drawing out the best of who that person is.

The type of change we are working for includes, but goes far beyond, intellectual understanding to encompass real, behavioral change—enabling people to continually build strong relationships through their communication.

We believe that we have done our most important work when we have empowered people to self-coach by connecting them with the purpose of each exercise we deliver and by opening their eyes to their own possibilities. People may garner a moment's applause through a "tips and tricks" approach to development but have no idea afterward what happened or how to continue achieving their best results. When people make progress through greater self-awareness, greater awareness of others, and a greater awareness of the dynamics of communication, they step into a universe of greatly expanded possibility.

From its three offices in Atlanta, New York, and San Francisco, Speakeasy works each year with some 4,500 executives and 350 client companies across five continents. We consistently have the privilege of developing an extraordinarily wide range of professionals—from young, high-potential executives to some of the most recognized names in business today. You can find out more about what we do and how we do it at **www.SpeakeasyInc.com**.

NOTES

1. Ann E. Tenbrunsel and David M. Messick, "Ethical Fading: The Role of Self-Deception in Unethical Behavior," *Social Justice Research*, Vol. 17, No. 2, June 2004.
2. Tenbrunsel and Messick, "Ethical Fading," 228.
3. "Sokal Hoax," *The Skeptic's Dictionary,* last modified August 11, 2011, accessed April 30, 2012, http://www.skepdic.com/sokal.html.
4. Lev Janashvili, "Lack of trust will force PR to rethink its methods," *PRWeek,* January 23, 2012, accessed May 1, 2012, http://www.prweekus.com/lack-of-trust-will-force-pr-to-rethink-its-methods/article/224126/.
5. "Record Decline in CEO Credibility," Edelman Trust Barometer, accessed April 30, 2012, http://trust.edelman.com/slides/japan-and-the-fragility-of-trust/.
6. "United Breaks Guitars," *Wikipedia,* last modified April 27, 2012, accessed April 30, 2012, http://en.wikipedia.org/wiki/United_Breaks_Guitars.
7. Weber Shandwick, *The Company Behind the Brand: In Reputation We Trust,* accessed May 1, 2012, available at http://www.webershandwick.com/resources/ws/flash/InRepWeTrust.pdf.
8. S. Rosen & A. Tesser, "On reluctance to communicate undesirable information: The MUM effect," *Sociometry* (1970), 33, 253-263.
9. Jim Collins, *Good to Great: Why Some Companies Make the Leap . . . and Others Don't* (New York: Harper Collins, 2001).
10. "Believe Me, I Have No Idea What I'm Talking About," Stanford Graduate School of Business, accessed December 28, 2011, http://www.stanford.edu/group/knowledgebase/cgi-bin/2009/10/20/believe-me-i-have-no-idea-what-i%e2%80%99m-talking-about/.

11. *Roger & Me.* Dir. Michael Moore, Dog Eat Dog Films, 1989.

12. Deloitte LLP 2010, "Ethics & Workplace Survey," Deloitte Development LLC, accessed December 15, 2011, http://www.deloitte.com/assets/Dcom-UnitedStates/Local%20Assets/Documents/us_2010_Ethics_and_Workplace_Survey_report_071910.pdf.

13. Chartered Institute of Personnel and Development, *Employee Outlook Survey*, October 2010. Full text available at http://www.cipd.co.uk/hr-resources/survey-reports/employee-outlook-autumn-2011.aspx.

14. Clare Churchard, "Employers Face Crisis of Trust in Management," http://www.peoplemanagement.co.uk/pm/articles/2011/10/employers-face-crisis-of-trust-in-management.htm, accessed December 29, 2011.

15. Scott Shane, Born Entrepreneurs, *Born Leaders: How Your Genes Affect Your Work Life* (Oxford University Press, 2010).

16. Jim Collins, "The Death of the Charismatic Leader," http://www.jimcollins.com/article_topics/articles/the-death-of-the-charismatic-leader.html.

17. Daniel Goleman, "What Makes a Great Leader," *Harvard Business Review,* November-December 1998, accessed May 1, 2012, http://www.theculturecoaches.com/images/what_makes_a_leader.pdf.

18. Jon Hamilton, "Think You're Multitasking? Think Again," NPR.org, October 2, 2008, accessed May 1, 2012, http://www.npr.org/templates/story/story.php?storyId=95256794.

19. Erick Shonfeld, "Forester Forecast: Online Retail Sales Will Grow to 250 Billion By 2014," Techcrunch.com, accessed January 18, 2012, http://techcrunch.com/2010/03/08/forrester-forecast-online-retail-sales-will-grow-to-250-billion-by-2014/.

20. Beyond Philosophy, Global Customer Management Experience Survey 2011; Full text available at http://beyondphilosophy.com/sites/default/files/2011-global-ce-management-survey.pdf.

21. Don Reisinger, "Apple Tops in Customer Satisfaction for 8th Year," CNET, September 19, 2011, accessed January 20, 2012, http://news.cnet.com/8301-13506_3-20108336-17/apple-tops-in-customer-satisfaction-for-8th-year/.

22. Brian Morrisey, "Q&A: Zappos CEO Tony Hsieh," *Adweek,* December

22, 2008, accessed February 10, 2012, http://www.adweek.com/news/advertising-branding/qa-zappos-ceo-tony-hsieh-97859?pn=2.

23. Marc Benioff, "Trust: A New Era of Business Value," Ethisphere, October 17, 2011, accessed May 2, 2012, http://www.ethisphere.com/trust-a-new-era-of-business-values-2/.

24. Quoted in Marc Benioff, "Trust"

25. Marc Benioff, "Trust."

26. James Surowiecki, "Are You Being Served?" *The New Yorker,* September 6, 2010.

27. Ann Pomeroy, "Great Communicators, Great Communication," *HR Magazine,* July 2006, accessed April 28, 2012, http://moss07.shrm.org/Publications/hrmagazine/EditorialContent/Pages/0706gptw_pomeroy.aspx.

28. Malcolm Gladwell, *The Tipping Point: How Little Things Can Make a Big Difference,* Little, Brown & Co, New York, 2000.

29. John Mackey, "Creating High Trust Organizations," *Huffington Post,* March 14, 2010, accessed May 3, 2012, http://www.huffingtonpost.com/john-mackey/creating-the-high-trust-o_b_497589.html.

30. Indra Nooyi, "The Best Advice I Ever Got," CNN Money, last modified April 30, 2008, accessed May 3, 2012, http://money.cnn.com/galleries/2008/fortune/0804/gallery.bestadvice.fortune/7.html.

31. David Cummings, personal interview, March 2012.

32. Coleman Breland, personal interview, March 2012.

33. "Sharp Drop in American Enthusiasm for Free Market, Poll Shows," Globescan.com, April 6, 2011, accessed May 1, 2012, http://www.globescan.com/commentary-and-analysis/press-releases/press-releases-2011/94-press-releases-2011/150-sharp-drop-in-american-enthusiasm-for-free-market-poll-shows.html.

34. Thomas B. Edsall, "Is This the End of Market Democracy?" *The New York Times,* February 19, 2012.

35. Robert Jensen, "Anti-Capitalism in Five Minutes," Counterpunch.org, April 30, 2001, accessed May 14, 2012, http://www.counterpunch.org/2007/04/30/anti-capitalism-in-five-minutes/.

36. In 2012 Edelman Trust Barometer Executive Summary, Richard Edelman, http://www.scribd.com/doc/79026497/2012-Edelman-Trust-Barometer-Executive-Summary.

37. Milton Friedman, "The Social Responsibility of Business is to Increase Profits," *New York Times Magazine,* September 13, 1970.

38. "JPMorgan Chase CEO: I Have No Idea Whether We Broke the Law," *Huffington Post,* May 11, 2012, accessed May 14, 2012, http://www.huffingtonpost.com/2012/05/11/jamie-dimon-i-have-no-idea-whether-we-broke-law_n_1510700.html.

39. Richard Branson, *Screw Business as Usual* (New York: Penguin Group, 2011), *17-18.*

40. An Interview with John Mackey, founder of Whole Foods, Grist.org, December 18, 2004, accessed May 5, 2012, http://grist.org/food/little-mackey/.

41. Samuel A. DiPiazza, Jr. and Robert G. Eccles, *Building Public Trust: The Future of Corporate Reporting* (New York: John Wiley & Sons, Inc., 2001).

42. Rachel Glennerster and Yongseok Shing, "Does Transparency Pay?" International Monetary Fund, Vol. 55, No. 1, 2008.

43. Jacquelyn Smith, "America's Most Trustworthy Companies," *Forbes,* March 20, 2012, accessed May 5, 2012, http://www.forbes.com/sites/jacquelynsmith/2012/03/20/americas-most-trustworthy-companies/.

INDEX

A

active listening, 110–11
advisors and counselors, 62–63
Alchemist, The (Coelho), 70–71
Amazon, 87
American Customer Satisfaction Index, 80
American Express, 125
Andersen, Erika, 73–74
Apple, 79–80
Atlanta Chamber of Commerce Board of Advisors Panel, 45–46
authentic self/authentic leadership, 9–11, 23–24, 56–57. See also communication; self-aware leaders

B

Baby Boomers, 2
Bass, Bernard M., 54
behavioral theories on leaders, 53–54, 56–57
Benioff, Marc, 86–87
Beyond Philosophy 2011 Global Customer Experience Management Survey, 79–80
Blanchard, Ken, 62
Bohm, David, 20
boycotts, 25, 36
Branson, Richard, 123–24
Breland, Coleman, 45–46, 116–17
British CIPD Employee Outlook Survey, 50–51
Building Public Trust (DiPiazza), 127
Burns, James MacGregor, 54
business, 119–32
    decline in trust in, 119–21
    and ethics, 22–23, 129–31
    marketing or advertising, 28, 41, 125–26
    profit pursuit vs. social responsibility, 121–25
    public relations, 12–15, 130
    role of communication, 108–9, 131–32
    serving the greater good, 126–29
    trust as critical value, 4
    See also corporate culture of trust; corporate toolbox (old style)

C

Capitalism 24902, 124
Carlyle, Thomas, 53
cause marketing, 125–26
Chambers, John, 60
"Charge of the Light Brigade, The" (Tennyson), 93
charisma, 55, 57
charismatic leaders, 55–57, 67
CIPD Employee Outlook Survey, 50–51
Cisco Systems, 98
coaching and mentoring, 63–65
Coelho, Paulo, 70–71
collaboration
    incentives for, 114–17, 118
    inclusion practices, 101–6, 117–18
    open communication aspect of, 96–101, 117
Collins, Jim, 48, 55–56
command and control business model, 93–95, 106
communication
    channel selection, 113–14
    in crises, 44–47
    diversity messaging, 104

euphemisms, 12, 15–18, 84–85
external, 12–15
feedback, 61–62, 98, 104–5
internal, 15–18
listening, 109–11
modeling authentic conversations, 108–9
one-on-one dialog with customers, 89
open communication vision, 96–101, 117
role of, 108–9, 131–32
self-deception and collusion in, 18–22
self-evaluation, 8–11
simple and sincere messages, 112–13
See also collaboration; customer service
communication technology
channel selection, 113–14
and command and control model, 94–95
and style for communicating, 112–13
utilizing the tools, 104–5, 113–14
See also internet
communication with employees, 39–52
DARE! opportunity, 51–52
expressing uncertainty, 47–49
and fear of "distracting" the workforce,
49–51
information brokering, 40–44
overview, 39–40
results of transparency, 44, 69–74, 128
sharing bad news, 44–47
compensation structure, employees' concerns
about, 41–44
Connectors in Chief, 101–6, 117–18
corporate culture of trust, 93–118
Connectors in Chief, 101–6, 117–18
DARE! opportunity, 117–18
institutional accountability, 126–29
open communication vision, 96–101, 117
overview, 93–96
rewards and recognition, 114–17, 118
See also business; collaboration;
communication; safety engineering
corporate toolbox (old style)
command and control model, 93–95, 106
credibility and confidence gap, 5, 29
deception and defensiveness, 11–12
euphemisms, 12, 15–18
"kissing up" culture, 20
strategy visions, 96
See also negative business practices
corporations, public view of, 26–27, 31

counselors and advisors, 62–63
Covey, Stephen R., 123
"Creating the High Trust Organization"
(Mackey), 106
credibility and confidence gap, 5, 29
crisis, communication during, 44–47
cultural differences, 107
Cummings, David, 111–12
Customer Choice Award, National Retail
Federation, 83–84
Customer Experience Management Survey,
Beyond Philosophy, 79–80
"Customer No-Service" (talk show), 78
customers, 25–37
DARE! opportunity, 36–37
default position, 27–32
emotions and connection to, 79–81, 89
overview, 25–26
"structural" distrust, 26–27
and transparency, 33–34, 85–88, 128
trust position, 32–36
See also public view
customer service, 77–92
costs vs. results, 79–81
customers' view of, 29–30, 34, 82–83, 88,
91–92
DARE! opportunity, 91–92
emotional connection, 79–81
executive awareness of, 88–89
faking sincerity vs. exceptional customer
service, 81–85
overview, 77–79
raising the bar, 89–90, 130
transparency, 85–88
cynicism, 2–3, 19–20

D

DARE! opportunities
about, 5–6
acknowledging your human vulnerability,
51–52
customer service, 91–92
examining your experiences as a consumer,
36–37
for self-aware leaders, 75–76
self-examination, 23–24
trusting corporate culture, 117–18
deception and defensiveness, 11–12

default position of customers, 27–32
Deloitte Consulting LLP, 50, 102–3
democratic free market capitalism, 119–22
devil's advocate, 62
Dimon, Jamie, 122
DiPiazza, Samuel, 127
dishonesty, 3, 99–101
Disraeli, Benjamin, 69
diversity messaging, 104

E

Earthwatch Australia, 97
economic system and scandals, 26
Edsall, Thomas B., 120–21
emotions
    allowing personal exposure to, 68–69,
        91–92
    and connection to customers, 79–81, 89
    empathetic understanding of others, 6,
        46–47, 69, 79
Employee Outlook Survey, British CIPD, 50–51
employees
    collusion/kissing up, 19–20
    and compensation structure, 41–44
    connectors of, 101–6, 117–18
    desire to serve a greater good, 125
    effect of deceit on, 12, 99–101
    motivations of, 48–49, 114–17, 118
    See also communication with employees
enlightened leadership, 22–24
ethical fading, 14
ethical revolution, 129–31
Ethics & Workplace Survey, Deloitte Consulting
    LLP, 50
Ethisphere Institute, 86
euphemisms, 12, 15–18, 84–85
expecting the best, 107
extrovert vs. introvert, 59–61

F

face time
    with customers, 89
    with employees, 105, 108–9
faking sincerity, 81–85, 99–101
fallacy of false choice, 123 24
fear of "distracting" the workforce, 49–51
feedback, 61–62, 98, 104–5

Forbes magazine, 87, 127
Forrester, 77–78
Fortune magazine, 107
free market, Americans' view of, 119–22
Friedman, Milton, 122

G

Gandhi, 72
Garber, Andy, 102–3
General Electric's ecomagination program, 124
generational differences, 2, 107
Giraudoux, Jean, 81
Gladwell, Malcolm, 101
globalization, 94, 122
GlobeScan, 120
GMI Ratings, One Hundred Most Trustworthy
    Companies, 127
Good to Great study (Collins), 48
Goodwork Project, Harvard University's, 2
Grand Circle Corp., 98
greater good, 125, 126–29
"Great Man" theory, 53. See also charismatic
    leaders

H

Harvard University's Goodwork Project, 2
Hayward, Tony, 44–45
honesty
    challenge to leaders, 6
    perception management vs., 12–15, 21–22
    restoration of, 3, 23–24
    and transparency, of self-aware leaders, 22,
        72–75, 76, 111–12, 128–29
    See also values
Howard, Clark, 78
Hsieh, Tony, 84
Hurricane Katrina, 103–4

I

incentives for collaboration, 114–17, 118
information
    brokering, 40–44
    credible sources, 28–29, 33
    top-down aspect of, 39 40
    See also communication; internet
internet

complaints via the, 30
effect on business, 94
online sales projections, 77–78
referrals from satisfied customers, 35
and transparency in customer interactions,
    85–86
Trust Sites, 86–87
See also communication technology
intimidation, 16–17
introvert vs. extrovert, 59–61
"Is this the End of Free Market Democracy?"
    (Edsall), 120–21

J

James, Carrie, 2
Janashvili, Lev, 26–27
J.D. Power's Smartphone Customer Satisfaction
    Survey, 80
Jefferson, Thomas, 57
Jensen, Robert, 121

K

Kabus, Al, 45–46
Kohl, David, 70–72
Kuusinen, Arto, 21–22

L

leaders, 53–76
    authentic self/authentic leadership, 9–11,
        23–24, 56–57
    customers' belief in credibility of, 29
    enlightened leadership, 22–24
    expressing uncertainty, 47–49
    face time, 89, 105, 108–9
    fear of "distracting" the workforce, 49–51
    and feedback, 61–62, 98, 104–5
    overview, 53–55
    responsibility for influencing corporate
        culture, 95–96
    setting the example, 66–67, 85, 105–6,
        108–11, 116–17
    sharing bad news, 44–47
    See also DARE! opportunities; self-aware
        leaders
"Leader's Edge, The" workshop, 8–11
leadership persona, 7–24
    author's experience, 8–11

charismatic, 55–57, 67
DARE! opportunity, 23–24
defensiveness and deception, 11–12
enlightened leadership, 22–23
extrovert vs. introvert, 59–61
obfuscation of morally questionable actions,
    15–18
overview, 7–8
perception management, 12–15, 21–22
self-deception and collusion, 18–22
Lewis, Alan, 98
Lincoln, Abraham, 66–67
Linver, Sandy, 10, 63–64
listening, 109–11
lying or asking someone to lie, 100

M

Mackey, John, 106, 124
Management By Walking Around (MBWA), 105
Mannes, Marya, 67
market economy, 119–22
marketing or advertising, 28, 41, 125–26
McCartney, Claire, 50–51
Menninger, Karl, 109
mentoring and coaching, 63–65
Messick, David, 14, 16
metaphors, 12, 15–18
Miller, Doug, 120
Miller, Earl, 65
Mitchell, Tony, 45–46
moderator of virtual meeting, 113
Moore, Michael, 49–50
Moore, Thomas, 108
"Most Admired Companies" (Forbes), 87
motivations of employees, 48–49, 114–17, 118
multitasking, 65–66
"Mum Effect," 44

N

narcissists, 68–69
National Retail Federation's Customer Choice
    Award, 83–84
negative business practices
    credibility and confidence gap, 5, 29
    cynicism, 2–3, 19–20
    deception and collusion, 11–12, 18–22,
        58–59

dishonesty, 3, 99–101
faking sincerity, 81–85, 99–101
intimidation, 16–17
obfuscation of morally questionable actions, 15–18
See also corporate toolbox (old style)
Nooyi, Indra, 107

O

obfuscation of morally questionable actions, 15–18
Occupy Wall Street movement, 120
O'Malley, Austin, 14
One Hundred Most Trustworthy Companies (GMI and Forbes), 127
open communication vision, 96–101, 117
Orwell, George, 23

P

Pamphile, Jo, 103–4
perception management, 12–15, 21–22
Perls, Fritz, 58
persona, 7–8, 21. See also leadership persona
personality assessments, 63
Pew Research Center, 3–4
Platt, Lew, 102
Polman, Paul, 121
positive intent, 107
profit motive vs. social responsibility, 121–25
psychometric testing, 63
public relations, 12–15, 130
public view
of corporations, 26–27, 31
of customer service, 29–30, 34, 82–83, 88, 91–92
of free market, 119–22
purpose-driven businesses, 125–26

R

recession, effect of, 26
referrals from satisfied customers, 34–35
rewards and recognition, 114–17, 118
Ricci, Ron, 59–61
Robinson, Rick, 46–47
Rockefeller, John D., 29
Roger & Me (documentary), 49–50
Russell, John, 88

S

safety engineering, 106–14
being yourself, 111–12
channel selection, 113–14
DARE! opportunity, 118
expecting the best, 107
listening, 109–11
modeling authentic conversations, 108–9
overview, 106–7
simple and sincere messages, 112–13
sales
canned vs. personal, 28, 29
contact employees, 29–30
customer trust position, 32–36
faking sincerity, 81
Faustian bargains, 87–88
online projections, 77–78
reputation of, 89–90
and transparency, 33–34, 86–87
See also customer service
Salesforce.com, 124
Screw Business as Usual (Branson), 123–24
secret strategies, 84–85
self-aware leaders
advisors and counselors, 62–63
coaches or mentors for, 63–65
DARE! opportunity, 75–76
enlightened leadership, 22–24
genuine feedback, 61–62, 98, 104–5
honesty and transparency, 22, 72–75, 76, 111–12, 128–29
making leaders of others, 116–17, 118
network of credible voices, 64–65
overview, 75
self-awareness, 57–61, 67–68
self-examination, 23–24
self-reflection, 65–68, 76, 110
vulnerability, 51–52, 68–72, 76
self-awareness, 57–61, 67–68
self-deception and collusion, 18–22, 58–59
self-examination, 23–24
self-reflection, 65–68, 76, 110
Shell's GroFin initiative, 124
Smartphone Customer Satisfaction Survey, J.D. Power's, 80
Smith, Adam, 121–22
social media, 104–5, 113–14
social responsibility
profit motive vs., 122–25

purpose-driven businesses, 125–26
    serving the greater good, 125, 126–29
sociopaths, 68–69
SoftCom, 97
Sokal, Alan, 16–17
Speakeasy, 4–5, 8–11, 113
Staubach, Roger, 83
"structural" distrust, 26–27

T

technology. See communication technology;
    internet
Tenbrunsel, Ann, 14, 16
Tennyson, Alfred, Lord, 93
theories about leaders, 53–55, 56–57
Thurber, James, 48
Tipping Point, The (Gladwell), 101
Tormala, Zakary, 48
trait theories on leaders, 53, 54, 55–57, 67
transactional theories on leaders, 54, 56–57
transformational leadership concept, 54
"Transgressing the Boundaries" (Sokal), 16–17
transparency
    and customers, 33–34, 85–88, 128
    and employees, 50–51, 128
    financial, 127–28
    and honesty, as leaders' value, 22, 72–75,
        76, 128–29
    overview, 6
    at Zappos, 84
    See also emotions; values
trust
    and communication with employees,
        40, 43–44
    crisis of, 1–3, 26–27
    customers' trust position, 32–36
    and employee's decision to find a
        different job, 50–51
    humans hardwired for, 32
    principles for building, 78–79
    rebuilding, 129–31
    responsibility from asking for, 51
    sociological benefits, 3–4
    See also corporate culture of trust;
        honesty; safety engineering;
        transparency; values
Trust.salesforce.com, 86–87
Trust Sites, 86–87

U

uncertainty, expressing, 48
Undercover Boss (TV program), 88
U.S. Congress approval ratings, 1

V

values
    authentic self/authentic leadership,
        9–11, 23–24, 56–57
    customers' awareness of, 35–36
    overview, 57
    See also honesty; self-aware leaders;
        transparency; trust
virtual meetings, 113–14
visioning open communication, 96–101, 117
vulnerability, 51–52, 68–72, 76

W

Wainewright, Phil, 86–87
Walton, Sam, 90
Wealth of Nations, The (Smith), 121–22
W Hotel, San Francisco, 81–82

Z

Zappos, 83–84